# Be prepared...
# To learn...
# To succeed...

# READY, SET, GO!

# NJ ASK
## Mathematics
## Grade 3

**Staff of Research & Education Association**
**Piscataway, New Jersey**

***Research & Education Association***
*Visit our website at*
**www.rea.com**

The Performance Standards in this book were created and implemented
by the New Jersey State Department of Education. For further information,
visit the Department of Education website at *www.state.nj.us/njded/cccs.*

**Research & Education Association**
61 Ethel Road West
Piscataway, New Jersey 08854
E-mail: info@rea.com

*Ready, Set, Go!*
**New Jersey ASK**
**Mathematics**
**Grade 3**

Printed in the United States of America

Library of Congress Control Number 2007922470

International Standard Book Number 0-7386-0283-3

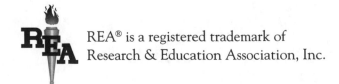

REA® is a registered trademark of
Research & Education Association, Inc.

# About Research & Education Association

Founded in 1959, Research & Education Association (REA) is dedicated to publishing the finest and most effective educational materials—including software, study guides, and test preps—for students in elementary school, middle school, high school, college, graduate school, and beyond.

Today REA's wide-ranging catalog is a leading resource for teachers, students, and professionals.

We invite you to visit us at *www.rea.com* to find out how "REA is making the world smarter."

# Acknowledgments

We would like to thank REA's Larry B. Kling, Vice President, Editorial, for supervising development; Pam Weston, Vice President, Publishing, for setting the quality standards for production integrity and managing the publication to completion; Molly Solanki, Associate Editor, for project management, editorial guidance, and preflight editorial review; Senior Editors Diane Goldschmidt, Anne Winthrop Esposito and Alice Leonard, for post-production quality assurance; Rachel DiMatteo, Graphic Artist, for her design contributions; Christine Saul, Senior Graphic Artist, for cover design; and Jeff LoBalbo, Senior Graphic Artist, for post-production file mapping.

We also gratefully acknowledge the writers, educators, and editors of REA and Northeast Editing for content development, editorial guidance, and final review. Thanks to Matrix Publishing for page design and typesetting.

# Contents

# Introduction

## Welcome to an Educational Adventure

The New Jersey Assessment of Skills and Knowledge, or NJ ASK, is the Garden State's answer to the federal No Child Left Behind Act, which requires that states use standards-based testing to ensure that students are picking up the skills and knowledge necessary for academic success.

We at REA believe that a friendly, hands-on introduction and preparation for the test are keys to creating a successful testing experience. REA's NJ ASK books offer these key features:

✓ Clearly identified book activities

✓ Contextual illustrations

✓ Easy-to-follow lessons

✓ Step-by-step examples

✓ Tips for solving problems tailored for the proper grade level

✓ Exercises to sharpen skills

✓ Real practice

Below is helpful information for students, parents, and teachers concerning the NJ ASK and test taking in general. Organized practice is itself a prime skill for young students to master, because it will help set the tone for success long into the future as their educational adventure continues. It is REA's sincere hope that this book—by providing relevant, standards-based practice—can become an integral part of that adventure.

## What is the NJ ASK?

The New Jersey Assessment of Skills and Knowledge is a standards-based assessment used in New Jersey's public schools. Performance on the NJ ASK test equates not with the grades students receive for teacher-assigned work but rather with proficiency measures pegged to how well students are acquiring the knowledge and skills outlined in the state's Core Curriculum Content Standards. Those proficiency measures fall into three broad categories, or bands: "partially proficient," "proficient," and "advanced proficient."

## When is the NJ ASK given?

The test is administered in early spring. Grade 3 students take the NJ ASK on three mornings, the first two in Language Arts Literacy, the final morning in Mathematics. Grade 4 students take the test on five mornings, the first two in Language Arts Literacy, the next two mornings in Mathematics, and the last in Science. Each morning's test spans 60 to 100 minutes, not including time to distribute materials, read directions, and take breaks.

## What is the format of the NJ ASK?

With multiple choice, students are asked to choose the correct answer out of four. With open-ended questions, children answer with written responses in their own words.

# Understanding the NJ ASK and This Book

## Students:

This book was specially written and designed to make test practice easy and fruitful for students. Our practice tests are very much like the actual NJ ASK tests, and our review is filled with illustrations, drills, exercises, and practice questions to help students become familiar with the testing environment and to retain information about key topics.

## Parents:

The NJ ASK and other state assessment tests are designed to give the school information about how well children are achieving in the areas required by New Jersey's Core Curriculum Content Standards. These standards describe what students should know at the end of certain grades. This book helps children review and prepare effectively and positively for the NJ ASK Mathematics.

## Teachers:

Teachers introduce students to the test-taking environment and the demands of the NJ ASK tests. Teachers can use our authoritative book in the classroom for planned, guided instruction and practice testing. Effective preparation means better test scores!

## Where can I obtain more information about the NJ ASK?

The New Jersey Department of Education offers four sources of information about the NJ ASK as follows:

www.state.nj.us/education

www.ets.org/njask

www.njpep.org/assessment

Office of Evaluation and Assessment
Telephone: 609-341-2456
Mailing address:
New Jersey Department of Education
PO Box 500
Trenton, NJ 08625-0500

## Test Accommodations and Special Situations

Every effort is made to provide a level playing field for students with disabilities who are taking the NJ ASK. Most students with educational disabilities and most students whose English language skills are limited take the standard NJ ASK. Students with disabilities will be working toward achieving the standards at whatever level is appropriate for them. Supports such as large-print type are available for students who have a current Individualized Education Program (IEP) or who have plans required under Section 504 or who use these supports and accommodations during other classroom testing.

If the IEP team decides that a student will not take the NJ ASK in Language Arts Literacy, Mathematics, and/or Science, the child will take the Alternate Proficiency Assessment (APA).

# Tips for Test Taking

- **Do your homework.** From the first assignment of the year, organize the day so there is always time to study and keep up with homework.

- **Communicate.** If there are any questions, doubts, or concerns about anything relating to school, study, or tests, speak up. This goes for teachers and parents, as well as students.

- **Get some rest.** Getting a good night's sleep the night before the test is essential to waking up sharp and focused.

- **Eat right.** Having a good breakfast—nothing very heavy—the morning of the test is what the body and mind need. Comfortable clothes, plenty of time to get to school, and the confidence of having prepared properly are all any student needs.

- **Test smart.** Read the questions carefully. Make sure answers are written correctly in the proper place on the answer sheet. Don't rush, and don't go too slow. If there is time, go back and check questions that you weren't sure about.

# Format and Scoring of the NJ ASK Mathematics

The questions on the NJ ASK can contain items and concepts learned in earlier grades. The tests are administered in March so that schools and parents receive the reports by mid-June. For third graders, the entire NJ ASK (including Math and Language Arts) <u>testing</u> takes place over three mornings. For both third and fourth graders the entire test ranges from about 60 minutes to 100 minutes of testing time per morning, not including time for distributing and collecting materials, reading directions, and giving breaks to students. For third graders, the Mathematics component of the test is given in one morning. Students have 83 minutes to complete the test. The school provides students with a calculator and a mathematics reference sheet that contains punch-out shapes and a ruler.

The NJ ASK Grade 3 Mathematics test contains a total of 30 test items. Twenty-seven of these items are multiple-choice, six of which are "non-calculator" multiple-choice items. The test also contains three open-ended questions.

Each multiple-choice question is worth 1 point, except for the non-calculator items, which are worth ½ point. The most a student can score on the multiple-choice questions is 24 points. Open-ended questions are worth 3 points each and are scored by using an item-specific rubric. The most a student can score on the three open-ended questions combined is 9 points. The highest score a student can receive on the NJ ASK Mathematics test is 33. Multiple-choice questions are scored by machine. Open-ended questions are scored by trained personnel.

Each test section is timed, and students may not proceed to the next section until time for the current section has expired. If students have not finished a section when time runs out, they must stop and put down their pencils. There are clear directions throughout the test.

# Core Curriculum Content Standards in Mathematics

The NJ ASK is not diagnostic, but is designed to measure how well students are achieving the NJ CCCS. The NJ CCCS determine what students should know and be able to do at certain grade levels. The NJ ASK assesses four Core Curriculum Content Standards in mathematics. The distribution of Standards in the test is as follows:

- 30.3% (10) of the points on the NJ ASK 3 assess Number and Numerical Operations

- 24.2% (8) of the points on the NJ ASK 3 assess Geometry and Measurement

- 24.2% (8) of the points on the NJ ASK 3 assess Patterns and Algebra

- 21.2% (7) of the points on the NJ ASK 3 assess Data Analysis, Probability, and Discrete Mathematics

Each standard of the CCCS has strands (see the following table) and Cumulative Progress Indicators (CPIs). All strands are tested on the NJ ASK, but not all CPIs are. The CPIs that coordinate with each strand are included here. For more information about the CPIs, access *www. nj.gov/njded/frameworks/math.*

## CCCS Mathematics Strands on the NJ ASK

| Standard | CCCS Strand | CPI | Chapter in This Book |
|---|---|---|---|
| Number and Numerical Operations | Number Sense | 4.1.3.A.1-6 | Chapter 1: Kinds of Numbers |
| | Numerical Operations | 4.1.3.B.1-7 | Chapter 2: Working with Numbers |
| | Estimation | 4.1.3.C.1-4 | Chapter 3: Estimation |
| Geometry and Measurement | Geometric Properties | 4.2.3.A.1-5 | Chapter 4: All About Lines and Shapes |
| | Transforming Shapes | 4,2,3,B.1-2 | Chapter 5: More About Shapes |
| | Coordinates of Geometry | 4.2.3.C.1 | Chapter 5: More About Shapes |
| | Units of Measurement | 4.2.3.D.1-3 | Chapter 6: Measuring |
| | Measuring Geometric Objects | 4.2.3.E.1-3 | Chapter 6: Measuring |
| Patterns and Algebra | Patterns and Relationships | 4.3.3.A.1 | Chapter 7: Understanding Patterns |
| | Functions | 4.3.3.B.1 | Chapter 7: Understanding Patterns |
| | Modeling | 4.3.3.C.1-2 | Chapter 7: Understanding Patterns |
| | Procedures | 4.3.3.D.1-2 | Chapter 7: Understanding Patterns |

| Data Analysis, Probability, and Discrete Mathematics | Data Analysis (statistics) | 4.4.3.A.1-2 | Chapter 8: Data Analysis and Probability |
| --- | --- | --- | --- |
| | Probability | 4.4.3.B.1-2 | Chapter 8: Data Analysis and Probability |
| | Discrete Mathematics—systematic listing and counting | 4.4.3.C.1-2 | Chapter 9: More About Analyzing Data |
| | Discrete Mathematics—vertex-edge graphs and algorithms | 4.4.3.D.1-3 | Chapter 9: More About Analyzing Data |

# Chapter 1

# Kinds of Numbers

You probably use numbers in speech and writing every day. You might tell your neighbor, "I have two sisters." Or maybe you promised your mother that you would do your homework in one hour. Perhaps you wrote down your telephone number for a friend.

Numbers are everywhere. We use numbers to stand for money and height. We even use numbers to tell time. Think of some other ways that we use numbers. Write two of these ways on the lines below.

_____

_____

In this chapter, you will learn about different kinds of numbers.

## Even and Odd Numbers

What do the numbers 2, 4, 6, 8, 10, and 12 have in common? They are even numbers. **Even numbers** end in 0, 2, 4, 6, or 8. Look at the number below. Think about whether it is even or odd.

258

Did you answer correctly? The number 258 ends in 8, so it's an even number.

**Odd numbers** end in 1, 3, 5, 7, or 9. The number 11 is an odd number. The number 327 is also an odd number.

Try this exercise for practice. Look at each of the numbers below.

**Circle the even numbers.**

3    15    18    32    56
121    298    300    478    589

How did you do? You should have circled 18, 32, 56, 298, 300, and 478.

Now, let's try another exercise.

**Circle the odd numbers.**

0    1    24    33    62
110    167    289    321    578

The odd numbers are 1, 33, 167, 289, and 321. Did you get them all?

# Practice Questions

## Practice 1: Even and Odd Numbers

**DIRECTIONS:**

Choose the best of the answer choices given for each of the following problems. Fill in the circle next to your choice.

1. Which number below is an even number?

   Ⓐ  197

   Ⓑ  278

   Ⓒ  1,203

   Ⓓ  1,327

Remember that an even number ends in 0, 2, 4, 6, or 8.

2. Which number below is an odd number?

   Ⓐ  28

   Ⓑ  132

   Ⓒ  150

   Ⓓ  313

Remember that an odd number ends in 1, 3, 5, 7, or 9.

# Whole Numbers

A **whole number** is an integer. An **integer** is a number on a number line. Zero is a whole number. Positive numbers are whole numbers. The numbers 1, 2, 3, 4, and 5 are positive numbers. Negative numbers are also integers. The numbers −1, −2, −3, −4, and −5 are negative numbers.

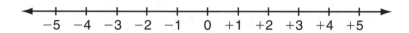

Not all numbers are whole numbers, however. Let's say that you eat one apple. You eat the whole thing. But then your little brother doesn't finish one half of his apple, so you eat it. You have now eaten one whole apple plus one half of an apple. In other words, you have eaten $1\frac{1}{2}$ apples. The number $1\frac{1}{2}$ is not a whole number. Numbers with fractions and decimals are not whole numbers.

# Place Value

The **place value** of each digit in a number is its value. The diagram below shows the place values for the digits in the number 100,000—one hundred thousand. Note that place values for whole numbers are assigned from the right to the left, beginning with the "ones."

```
hundred thousand
  ten thousand
    thousand
      hundred
        ten
          one

1   0   0,  0   0   0
```

Look at this number:

246

In this number, the 6 is in the ones place, the 4 is in the tens place, and the 2 is in the hundreds place. Notice how the places are assigned from right to left.

Now look at this number:

7,310

In this number, the 0 is in the ones place, the 1 is in the tens place, the 3 is in the hundreds place, and the 7 is in the thousands place.

Now look at a much larger number:

123,645

In this number, the 5 is in the ones place, the 4 is in the tens place, the 6 is in the hundreds place, the 3 is in the thousands place, the 2 is in the ten thousands place, and the 1 is in the hundred thousands place.

# Practice Questions

## Practice 2: Whole Numbers and Place Value

**DIRECTIONS:**

Choose the best of the answer choices given for each of the following problems. Fill in the circle next to your choice.

1.  The population of Newark, New Jersey, is 277,911. What is the value of the 9 in the number 277,911?

    Ⓐ   9 thousands

    Ⓑ   9 hundreds

    Ⓒ   9 tens

    Ⓓ   9 ones

 **HINT**

> If you're having trouble answering this question, go back and look at the diagram of the number 100,000. Find the place value of the third zero from the right. This will be the correct answer.

2.  The highest point in New Jersey is 1,803 feet. What is the value of the 1 in the number 1,803?

    Ⓐ   1 thousand

    Ⓑ   1 hundred

    Ⓒ   1 ten

    Ⓓ   1 one

 **HINT**

> If you're unsure, go back and look at the diagram showing place value. It might also help to count over from the right: ones, tens, hundreds, thousands.

# Fractions

**Fractions** stand for parts of a number. They are not whole.

The top and bottom of a fraction have special names. The top of a fraction is called the **numerator**. The bottom of a fraction is called the **denominator**. An easy way to remember this is to remember that the **d**enominator goes **d**own at the bottom of the fraction. A fraction tells how many parts of something you have. The *total* number of parts goes on the bottom. It is the denominator. The number of parts *you* have goes on the top. It is the numerator.

Look at the fractions below. Even if a fraction has a whole number in front of it, such as $1\frac{1}{4}$, it isn't a whole number. If a number has a whole number and a fraction, it is called a mixed fraction.

$$\frac{1}{2} \qquad \frac{1}{4} \qquad \frac{3}{4} \qquad 1\frac{1}{4} \qquad 2\frac{3}{4}$$

Suppose your family ordered a pizza with six slices.

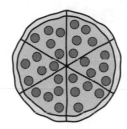

The pizza has six slices, so six is the denominator. In this case, the denominator tells how many slices of pizza make up the whole pizza. Now imagine that you ate one slice of pizza. You ate one part of the pizza. The fraction showing how much of the pizza you ate is $\frac{1}{6}$.

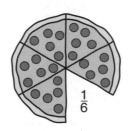

Look at the following numbers.

**Circle the whole numbers.**

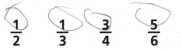

Did you get them all? You should have circled 1, 7, 10, 45, and 125.

Let's try another question:

**Circle the numerator in each of the fractions below.**

$$\frac{1}{2} \quad \frac{1}{3} \quad \frac{3}{4} \quad \frac{5}{6}$$

You should have circled 1, 1, 3, and 5 in the four numbers above. If you missed one or more, review the section on fractions.

# Practice Questions

## Practice 3: Fractions

**DIRECTIONS:**

**Choose the best of the answer choices given for each of the following problems. Fill in the circle next to your choice.**

1. **Which number below is a whole number?**

   Ⓐ  $\frac{1}{3}$

   Ⓑ  $2\frac{1}{5}$

   Ⓒ  $\frac{1}{4}$

   Ⓓ  312

HINT

Remember that fractions show parts of numbers.

2. **Which number below is a fraction?**

   Ⓐ  .999

   Ⓑ  2.34

   Ⓒ  $\frac{5}{12}$

   Ⓓ  450

HINT

Remember that a fraction has a numerator and a denominator.

# Which Is Greater?

Sometimes you might want to compare fractions to see which one is greater. If the denominators are the same, this is easy to do. If the denominators are the same, the fraction with the larger numerator is the greatest. For example, $\frac{5}{7}$ is greater than $\frac{4}{7}$.

If the denominators are different, however, it is harder to tell which fraction is larger. If you have a diagram with shaded parts, you can usually see which fraction is larger.

For example, look at the shaded blocks below.

 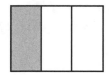

By looking at the blocks, you can see that $\frac{1}{2}$ is definitely greater than $\frac{1}{3}$.

Look at the fractions below. On the line below the fractions, put them in order from GREATEST to LEAST. Use the shaded diagrams to help you.

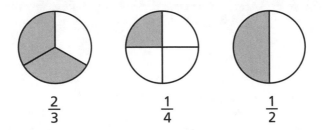

$\frac{2}{3}$ $\frac{1}{4}$ $\frac{1}{2}$

If you said the order is $\frac{2}{3}$, $\frac{1}{2}$, $\frac{1}{4}$ from greatest to least, you are right.

## Equivalent Fractions

Some fractions stand for the same amount even though they have different numerators and denominators. These are called **equivalent fractions**. Look at the fractions $\frac{2}{4}$ and $\frac{1}{2}$.

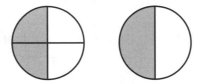

$\frac{2}{4}$ is equivalent to $\frac{1}{2}$.

Compare the fractions below. Write < (less than), > (greater than), or = (equal to) for each pair of fractions. Use the shaded circles to help you choose the right answer.

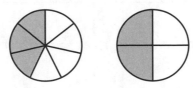

1. $\frac{3}{7}$ ⬚ $\frac{2}{4}$

2. $\frac{4}{5}$ ◁ $\frac{7}{8}$

3. $\frac{3}{4}$ ⊠ $\frac{2}{3}$

4. $\frac{1}{2}$ ▱ $\frac{5}{10}$

The answers should be

1. $<$

2. $<$

3. $>$

4. $=$

# Practice Questions

## Practice 4: Comparing Fraction Sizes

**DIRECTIONS:**

Choose the best of the answer choices given for each of the following problems. Fill in the circle next to your choice.

1.  **Compare the shaded regions. Which symbol belongs in the box?**

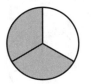 

$$\frac{2}{3} \; \boxed{} \; \frac{1}{2}$$

Ⓐ  <

Ⓑ  >

Ⓒ  =

Ⓓ  None of the above

**HINT**

See whether the shaded area in the first circle is bigger than the shaded area in the second circle. If it is, choose the answer option with the greater than (>) sign.

2. **Compare the shaded regions. Which symbol belongs in the box?**

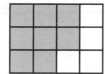 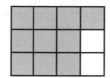

$\frac{8}{12}$  $\frac{10}{12}$

Ⓐ  <

Ⓑ  >

Ⓒ  =

Ⓓ  None of the above

**HINT**

Count the blocks. Then see if the shaded area in the first picture has more or fewer boxes shaded than the second.

# Decimals

**Decimals** also stand for parts of numbers. A decimal has a **point**. The numbers to the right of the point show the part of the number. The number below is a decimal.

.25

Sometimes there are also numbers to the left of the decimal. Look at this number.

3.25

This number contains the whole number 3. But because of the .25, it isn't a whole number. It is called a mixed decimal because it has a whole number part and a decimal part.

Like whole numbers, decimals have place values. But the place values for decimals are counted from the decimal point from left to right. Notice that "th" is added to the end of each place value for decimals, and there is no place value for one—they start at tenths.

Look at the diagram below.

Now look at this decimal.

.31

Write the value of the digit 1 in this number on the line below. Use the diagram above for .54 to help you.

_____

If you said the 1 in .31 is in the hundredths place, you are right. If you thought it was something else, review the place value diagram for .54 above.

# Practice Questions

## Practice 5: Decimals

**DIRECTIONS:**

Choose the best of the answer choices given for each of the following problems. Fill in the circle next to your choice.

1. **For the number, .98, what is the value of the 8?**

   Ⓐ   8 tens

   Ⓑ   8 hundreds

   Ⓒ   8 tenths

   Ⓓ   8 hundredths

HINT

Use the place value diagram if you need help. Remember to add the "th" to the place values for decimals.

2. **For the number .34, what is the value of the 3?**

   Ⓐ   3 tens

   Ⓑ   3 hundreds

   Ⓒ   3 tenths

   Ⓓ   3 hundredths

HINT

Remember that there isn't a ones place after a decimal point. It begins with tenths.

# Practice Questions

## End-of-Chapter Practice Problems

**DIRECTIONS:**

Choose the best of the answer choices given for each of the following problems. Fill in the circle next to your choice.

1. **Compare the shaded regions. Which symbol belongs in the box?**

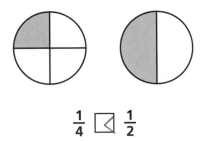

  Ⓐ  <

  Ⓑ  >

  Ⓒ  =

  Ⓓ  None of the above

HINT

Look carefully at the shaded regions. Is the first one bigger or smaller than the second?

2.  **The population in Julio's city is 128,543. What is the value of the 2 in the number 128,543?**

    Ⓐ  20 thousands

    Ⓑ  2 thousands

    Ⓒ  20 hundreds

    Ⓓ  2 hundreds

 **HINT**

> If you don't know the value of the 2, turn back and look at the place value diagram in the chapter.

3.  **Which number below is an odd number?**

    Ⓐ  10

    Ⓑ  36

    Ⓒ  45

    Ⓓ  202

 **HINT**

> Try to remember the numbers that an odd number ends in. If you can't, turn back to the discussion of even and odd numbers in the chapter.

4.  **Which number below is a fraction?**

    Ⓐ  2.34

    Ⓑ  $\frac{1}{5}$

    Ⓒ  32

    Ⓓ  1,864

 **HINT**

> Try to remember what a fraction looks like. How is it different from a whole number or a decimal?

5. **Compare the shaded regions. Which symbol belongs in the box?**

$$\frac{1}{4} \; \square \; \frac{1}{3}$$

    Ⓐ   <

    Ⓑ   >

    Ⓒ   =

    Ⓓ   None of the above

**HINT**

Look carefully at the shaded regions. Which one is greater?

6. **For the number .25, what is the value of the 5?**

    Ⓐ   5 tenths

    Ⓑ   5 tens

    Ⓒ   5 hundreds

    Ⓓ   5 hundredths

**HINT**

If you can't remember the place value for a decimal, turn back to the discussion of decimal place values in the chapter.

7.  **Which number below is a decimal?**

    Ⓐ  1.45

    Ⓑ  .19

    Ⓒ  $\frac{3}{5}$

    Ⓓ  405

HINT

What does a decimal have that a fraction and a whole number do not?

8.  **Compare the fractions. Which symbol belongs in the box?**

    $$\frac{6}{7} \;\square\; \frac{3}{7}$$

    Ⓐ  <

    Ⓑ  >

    Ⓒ  =

    Ⓓ  None of the above

HINT

Remember that when fractions have the same denominator, the fraction with the greater numerator is larger.

9.  Keisha lives 2,710 miles from her grandmother. What is the value of 7 in the number 2,710?

Ⓐ  7 thousandths

Ⓑ  7 hundreds

Ⓒ  7 tens

Ⓓ  7 ones

Remember that the places in whole numbers are assigned from right to left, starting with ones, then tens, then hundreds, and so forth.

10. **Which number below is an even number?**

Ⓐ  212

Ⓑ  315

Ⓒ  1,079

Ⓓ  2,001

Try to remember which numbers are at the end (ones place) for even numbers. If you can't remember, turn back to the discussion of even and odd numbers in the chapter.

# Chapter 2

# Working with Numbers

72 x 5 =

In Chapter 1, you learned about different kinds of numbers. You learned that numbers can be whole, and that whole numbers can be even or odd. You learned about fractions and decimals, and you learned about place values for both whole numbers and decimals.

In this chapter, you'll learn how to answer **addition** and **subtraction** questions. You'll also learn how to answer multiplication and division questions. You'll notice that some test questions on the test are easier to answer than others. You'll be able to answer the easier questions by using **mental math**. When you use mental math, you figure out the answer in your head. For other questions, you'll have to use paper and pencil to figure out the answer.

The NJ ASK test is given in sessions. For some sessions, you will be allowed to use a calculator. For other sessions, you are not allowed to use a calculator. In this chapter, you'll practice answering questions both ways.

## Adding and Subtracting Numbers

You can use mental math to solve some questions about numbers. For example, you should be able to answer the following question quickly by using mental math.

**Find the exact answer: 100 + 50**

    Ⓐ  50

    Ⓑ  100

    Ⓒ  150

    Ⓓ  510

The number 100 added to 50 is 150. Answer choice C is the correct answer. Let's try another.

**Find the exact answer: 200 − 100**

    Ⓐ  50

    Ⓑ  100

    Ⓒ  200

    Ⓓ  300

This question can also be solved easily by using mental math. You should know right away that 200 − 100 is 100. Answer choice B is correct.

Not all problems can be solved this quickly, however. Try to solve this problem:

**Find the exact answer: 132 + 42 + 10**

    Ⓐ  174

    Ⓑ  180

    Ⓒ  184

    Ⓓ  194

$$\begin{array}{r} 132 \\ +\,42 \\ \hline 174 \\ +\,10 \\ \hline 184 \end{array}$$

You probably can't solve this problem right away in your head. If you are not allowed to use a calculator, you'll need to use a pencil and paper. Set up the problem like this:

$$
\begin{array}{r}
132 \\
42 \\
+\ \ 10 \\
\hline
\end{array}
$$

When you set up the problem this way, it's easy to add the numbers. You can tell that the correct answer choice is C, 184.

Let's try another.

**Find the exact answer: 76 – 54**

    Ⓐ  20

    Ⓑ  22

    Ⓒ  24

    Ⓓ  26

You'll probably need a pencil and paper to answer this problem, too. If you use a pencil and paper, set up the problem this way:

$$
\begin{array}{r}
76 \\
-\ \ 54 \\
\hline
\end{array}
$$

If you set up the problem this way, you can easily subtract the numbers and get 22 (answer choice B). Now use a calculator to solve the problem. Press the keys for 7 and 6 and then press the minus sign. Then press the keys for 54 and press the = sign. The answer 22 shows up on the screen.

Let's try a word problem now.

**Enrico has a bag of jelly beans. He has 26 orange jelly beans, 32 green jelly beans, and 12 red jelly beans. How many jelly beans does he have in all?**

    Ⓐ   58

    Ⓑ   68

    Ⓒ   70

    Ⓓ   72

If you use a pencil and paper to solve this problem, set it up like this:

$$
\begin{array}{r}
^1\ \ \\
26 \\
32 \\
+\ 12 \\
\hline
70
\end{array}
$$

Don't forget to carry the 1 when you add the first row of numbers on the right. Your answer should be 70. Answer choice C is correct.

Also practice solving this problem using a calculator. Press 26 + 32 + 12 and then press =.

# Practice Questions

## Practice 6: Adding and Subtracting Numbers

**DIRECTIONS:**

**Choose the best of the answer choices given for each of the following problems. Fill in the circle next to your choice. You may NOT use a calculator.**

1. **Find the exact answer: 80 + 20**

   Ⓐ 60

   Ⓑ 80

   ● 100

   Ⓓ 110

 **HINT**

You should be able to use mental math to solve this problem.

2. **Find the exact answer: 100 − 30**

   Ⓐ 60

   ● 70

   Ⓒ 75

   Ⓓ 80

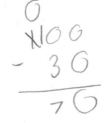

$$\begin{array}{r} \overset{0}{\cancel{10}0} \\ -\ 30 \\ \hline 70 \end{array}$$

 **HINT**

Use mental math to solve this problem, too.

3.  Sarah has taken three math tests. She scored 82, 79, and 90 points on the tests. How many points does she have in all?

Ⓐ 200

Ⓑ 251

Ⓒ 252

Ⓓ 261

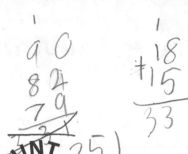

HINT

Use a pencil and paper to solve this problem. Set up the problem as we did earlier, so it's easier to add the numbers.

4.  Find the exact answer: 190 + 45 + 62

Ⓐ 197

Ⓑ 290

Ⓒ 297

Ⓓ 397

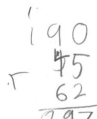

HINT

Set up this problem so it's easy to add the numbers by using pencil and paper.

5.  Julie has 35 pencils. She gives 10 to her sister and 15 to her friend. How many pencils does she have left?

     Ⓐ   5

     Ⓑ   10

     Ⓒ   15

     Ⓓ   20

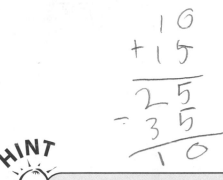

HINT

An easy way to solve this problem is to add 10 and 15 and then subtract this number from 35.

# Multiplying and Dividing Numbers

On the NJ ASK, you'll be asked to **multiply** and **divide** numbers. For some of these problems, you'll be allowed to use a calculator. For others, you'll need to use a pencil and paper or mental math.

**Find the exact answer: 144 ÷ 12**

     Ⓐ   8

     Ⓑ   1

     Ⓒ   12

     Ⓓ   14

HINT

To solve this problem using a calculator, press the keys for 144, then press ÷, and then press 12 and the = sign. The answer is 12, so answer choice C is correct.

If you are not allowed to use a calculator, set up the problem like this:

$$12\overline{)144}$$

Let's try another one:

**Find the exact answer: 15 × 3**

    Ⓐ  18

    Ⓑ  30

    Ⓒ  45

    Ⓓ  60

HINT

You might be able to solve this problem by using mental math. To solve it using a calculator, press the keys for 15 and the × sign. Then press 3 and the = sign. The answer is 45. Answer choice C is the correct answer. To solve this problem using a pencil and paper, set it up like this:      15
                                                  × 3

Let's try one more:

There are 24 students in Jamal's class. Jamal would like to give each student 3 stickers. How many stickers does he need?

Ⓐ  27

Ⓑ  48

Ⓒ  60

Ⓓ  72

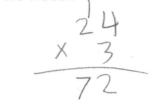

**HINT**

If you can use a calculator to solve this problem, press the keys for 24 and then press the × sign. Then press the 3 key and the = key. The answer is 72. Answer choice D is correct. If you can't use a calculator, set up the problem like this:     24
                                                                                                          × 3

# Practice Questions

## Practice 7: Multiplying and Dividing Numbers

**DIRECTIONS:**

Choose the best of the answer choices given for each of the following problems. Fill in the circle next to your choice. You may NOT use a calculator.

**1.  Find the exact answer: 90 ÷ 9**

Ⓐ  3

Ⓑ  5

Ⓒ  9

Ⓓ  10

**HINT**

You should be able to do this problem in your head. Think about multiplication. What number multiplied by 9 equals 90?

2.  Find the exact answer: 14 × 8

    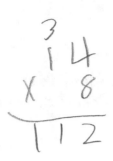

    Ⓐ  22

    Ⓑ  84

    Ⓒ  98

    ● 112

HINT

Set up the problem like this:       14
                                  ×  8

**DIRECTIONS:**

You are allowed to use a calculator to answer the following multiple-choice item.

3.  Tara is planning a special lunch for her mother's birthday. She would like to give each of the 18 guests 3 flowers. How many flowers does she need?

    Ⓐ  21

    ● 54

    Ⓒ  72

    Ⓓ  180

HINT

To solve this problem, multiply 18 by 3.

# Counting Money

Do you like to count money? We'll review **counting money**—adding and subtracting coins—in this section. Most questions about money involve **coins**—nickels, dimes, and quarters. You need to know the value of these coins to answer these questions.

 5¢

 10¢

 25¢

Let's try a **money question**:

**Marcy would like to buy a pen that costs $1.25. She gives the clerk $1.50. How much change will she receive?**

    Ⓐ  10¢

    Ⓑ  20¢

    Ⓒ  25¢

    Ⓓ  30¢

 HINT

Subtract $1.25 from $1.50. Marcy should receive 25¢ change.

Some questions on the NJ ASK are **open-ended**. This means you have **to show your work** and come up with an answer on your own. Let's try one of these questions:

**A machine charges 85¢ for a bottle of water and accepts only nickels, dimes, and quarters. The machine requires exact change.**

**What combination of coins could you put in the machine to get a bottle of water?**

**Show your work or explain your answer.**

You can answer this question two different ways. You can draw pictures of the coins or write out the coins that you would need. Of course, there are several combinations of coins that you could use. You could say, "I would use 3 quarters (75¢) and 1 dime (10¢)." You could also say that you would use 2 nickels instead of the dime. Yet another way is to use 2 quarters (50¢), 3 dimes (30¢), and 1 nickel (5¢). As long as your coins add up to 85¢, your answer is right!

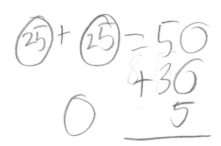

$$25 + 25 = 50$$
$$+ 30$$
$$0 \quad 5$$

Let's try one more counting money problem:

**To park his car for an hour, Mr. Bretton has to put 55¢ in a meter. This meter accepts only quarters, dimes, and nickels. Which combination of coins should he put in the meter?**

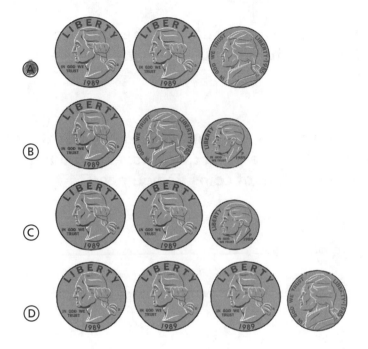

Ⓐ

Ⓑ

Ⓒ

Ⓓ

**HINT**

Add up each of the coins in each answer choice. Choose the one that adds up to 55¢. Answer choice A is the only one that adds up to 55¢, so this is the correct answer.

# Practice Questions

## Practice 8: Counting Money

**DIRECTIONS:**

Choose the best of the answer choices given for each of the following problems. Fill in the circle next to your choice. You are allowed to use a calculator to answer these items.

1. To attend a basketball game at your school, you have to pay 65¢ to get in. The school accepts only nickels, dimes, and quarters, and you must have exact change. Which combination of coins do you need?

Remember that the value of two quarters is 50¢.

2. A pinball machine charges 35¢ for a game and accepts only nickels, dimes, and quarters. The machine requires exact change.

   What combination of coins could you put in the machine to play a game?

   Show your work or explain your answer.

Remember that a quarter has a value of 25¢, a dime has a value of 10¢, and a nickel has a value of 5¢.

# Practice Questions

## End-of-Chapter Practice Problems

**DIRECTIONS:**

Choose the best of the answer choices given for each of the following problems. Fill in the circle next to your choice. You may NOT use a calculator.

1. Find the exact amount: 210 + 80

   Ⓐ 270

   Ⓑ 280

   Ⓒ 290

   Ⓓ 300

Use mental math to solve this problem.

**2. Find the exact answer: 128 ÷ 8**

Ⓐ 6

Ⓑ 8

Ⓒ 12

Ⓓ 16

**HINT**
When you divide, remember that $8 \times 6 = 48$.

**3. Lisa has 34 blue marbles, 28 green marbles, and 25 white marbles. How many marbles does she have in all?**

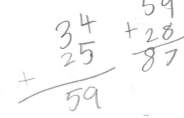

Ⓐ 75

Ⓑ 78

Ⓒ 85

Ⓓ 87

**HINT**
Remember to carry the 1 in the first row.

**4. Ray has 108 baseball cards that he wants to give to his 18 friends. How many baseball cards will he give to each friend?**

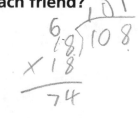

Ⓐ 6

Ⓑ 8

Ⓒ 10

Ⓓ 18

**HINT**
You have to divide 18 into 108 to solve this problem.

5. A country fair charges 75¢ to get in and accepts only nickels, dimes, and quarters. The fair requires exact change.

   What combination of coins could you use to get into the fair?

   Show your work or explain your answer.

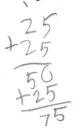

   > **HINT**
   >
   > Remember that a quarter has a value of 25¢. Choose the combination of coins that is easiest to add.

6. **Find the exact answer: 72 × 6**

   Ⓐ 78

   Ⓑ 360

   Ⓒ 430

   Ⓓ 432

   > **HINT**
   >
   > Sct up the numbers so it's easy to multiply them.

7. **Rose has 40 sheets of paper. She uses 12 sheets and gives 22 sheets to her friend. How many sheets of paper does Rose have left?**

   Ⓐ 2

   Ⓑ 4

   Ⓒ 6

   Ⓓ 8

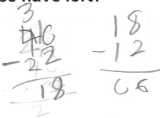

   > **HINT**
   >
   > Subtract 12 and 22 from 40.

8. Cara would like to buy a bottle of juice that costs 89¢. She gives the clerk $1.00. How much change will she receive?

Ⓐ  9¢

Ⓑ  10¢

Ⓒ  11¢

Ⓓ  12¢

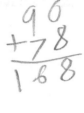

**HINT**

> Subtract 89¢ from 100¢. Note that one dollar is the same value as 100¢.

9. Find the exact amount: 22 + 56 + 90

Ⓐ  158

Ⓑ  162

Ⓒ  168

Ⓓ  169

**HINT**

> Remember to set up the numbers so that they are easy to add.

10. Find the exact amount: 500 − 75

Ⓐ  375

Ⓑ  400

Ⓒ  425

Ⓓ  450

**HINT**

> Use mental math to solve this problem.

# Chapter 3

# Estimation

How long do you think it will take you to finish reading this chapter? You don't know for sure, because you just started. But you could probably **estimate**—or guess—how long it would take.

Sometimes you don't have to come up with an exact answer to a question. An estimate will do. For these questions, you make an educated guess at the answer. Remember how most of the questions in Chapter 2 asked you to find the exact answer? Your answer won't be exact when you estimate, but it will be close to the exact answer. You will NOT be allowed to use a calculator for estimation questions on the NJ ASK test.

## Rounding

You can use **mental math** to answer some estimation questions. Do you remember what mental math is? It's when you figure out the answer in your head without using a pencil and paper or a calculator.

For most estimation questions, **rounding** numbers is usually the best way to estimate. You can round numbers to the nearest 10 or the nearest 100. When you round to the nearest 10, you look closely at the number in the ones place. For the number 23, for example, 3 is in the ones place. If the number in the ones place is 5 or more, you round up. If the number is 4 or less, you round down. Since the number 3 is less than 5, you round down. The number 23 rounded to the nearest 10 is 20. See how it works?

The numbers below are rounded to the nearest 10.

| Number | Rounded to Nearest 10 |
|:------:|:---------------------:|
| 34 | 30 |
| 67 | 70 |
| 78 | 80 |
| 91 | 90 |

Now you try rounding. Round each of the following numbers to the nearest 10.

| Number | Rounded to Nearest 10 |
|:------:|:---------------------:|
| 11 | _10_ |
| 15 | _20_ |
| 24 | _20_ |
| 37 | _40_ |
| 42 | _40_ |
| 59 | _60_ |
| 65 | _70_ |

The correct answers are 10, 20, 20, 40, 40, 60, and 70.

Similarly, when you round the nearest hundred, you look closely at the number in the tens place. If this number is 5 or greater, you round up. If this number is 4 or less, you round down. These numbers are rounded to the nearest hundred:

| Number | Rounded to Nearest 100 |
|--------|------------------------|
| 123 | 100 |
| 182 | 200 |
| 214 | 200 |
| 356 | 400 |
| 479 | 500 |
| 591 | 600 |

Now you try it.

| Number | Rounded to Nearest 100 |
|--------|------------------------|
| 115 | 100 |
| 179 | 200 |
| 234 | 200 |
| 390 | 400 |
| 450 | 500 |
| 625 | 600 |

The answers are 100, 200, 200, 400, 500, and 600.

# Estimating Addition

When you estimate addition problems, your answer options will be in a **range**. A range has two numbers. The exact sum is somewhere between these two numbers. The **sum** is the number you get when you add two numbers together. You can estimate addition by rounding the original numbers and adding these rounded numbers.

The problem below is a typical question for estimating a sum:

**Estimate 124 + 82. The sum is between which numbers?**

  Ⓐ   100 and 299

  Ⓑ   300 and 499

  Ⓒ   500 and 699

  Ⓓ   700 and 899

To answer this problem, you need to round 124 to the nearest hundred. It's 100. Then round 82 to the nearest 10. That's 80. Now add these numbers together. You get 180. The number 180 is between 100 and 299, so answer choice A is correct. Let's try another one.

**Estimate 215 + 390. The sum is between which numbers?**

  Ⓐ   100 and 199

  Ⓑ   300 and 499

  Ⓒ   500 and 699

  Ⓓ   700 and 899

Round 215 to the nearest hundred. It's 200. Now round 390 to the nearest hundred. It's 400. Add these two numbers together: 200 + 400 = 600. Answer choice C gives a range of between 500 and 699. The number 600 is in this range, so this is the correct answer.

# Practice Questions

## Practice 9: Estimating Addition

**DIRECTIONS:**

Choose the best of the answer choices given for each of the following problems. Fill in the circle next to your choice. You may NOT use a calculator.

1. **Estimate 256 + 64. The sum is between which numbers?**

   Ⓐ   100 and 200

   Ⓑ   201 and 300

   ⬤   301 and 400

   Ⓓ   401 and 500

   **HINT**
   > Round 256 to the nearest hundred. Then round 60 to the nearest 10. Then add the two numbers together.

2. **Estimate 120 + 471. The sum is between which numbers?**

   Ⓐ   100 and 299

   Ⓑ   300 and 499

   ⬤   500 and 699

   Ⓓ   700 and 899

   **HINT**
   > Round 120 to the nearest hundred. Then round 471 to the nearest hundred. Then add the two numbers together.

# Estimating Subtraction

You estimate subtraction just like you estimate addition. Again, estimation questions ask you to choose a **correct range** of numbers. For subtraction, however, you'll look for the **difference** instead of the sum. Let's try this one:

**Estimate 999 − 204. The difference is between which numbers?**

    Ⓐ  1,300 and 1,500

    Ⓑ  1,000 and 1,200

    Ⓒ  700 and 900

    Ⓓ  400 and 600

To answer this question, round 999 to the nearest *thousand*, since it is only one number away from 1,000. Then round 204 to the nearest hundred. This is 200. If you subtract 200 from 1,000, you get 800. Answer choice C is correct.

Let's try another problem.

**Estimate 280 − 150. The difference is between which numbers?**

    Ⓐ  100 and 299

    Ⓑ  300 and 499

    Ⓒ  500 and 699

    Ⓓ  700 and 899

Round both of these numbers to the nearest hundred. When you round 280 to the nearest hundred, you get 300. The number 150 rounded to the nearest hundred is 200. When you subtract 200 from 300, you get 100. Answer choice A is correct.

# Practice Questions

## Practice 10: Estimating Subtraction

**DIRECTIONS:**

Choose the best of the answer choices given for each of the following problems. Fill in the circle next to your choice. You may NOT use a calculator.

1. **Estimate 520 − 92. The difference is between which numbers?**

   (A) 100 and 299

   (B) 300 and 499

   (C) 500 and 699

   (D) 700 and 899

   $$\begin{array}{r} 500 \\ -\ 100 \\ \hline 400 \end{array}$$

   **HINT**

   Round 520 to the nearest hundred. Then round 92 to the nearest ten. Then subtract the numbers, and choose the correct answer.

2. **Estimate 980 − 670. The difference is between which numbers?**

   (A) 1,300 and 1,500

   (B) 1,000 and 1,200

   (C) 700 and 900

   (D) 200 and 400

   $$\begin{array}{r} 1000 \\ -\ 700 \\ \hline 300 \end{array}$$

   **HINT**

   Begin by rounding both numbers to the nearest hundred. Then subtract the second number from the first. Then choose the right range.

# Estimating Multiplication

You might be asked to estimate multiplication problems on the NJ ASK. For multiplication problems, you'll estimate the product. The **product** is the number you get when you multiply two numbers together. Rounding will help you estimate the product. Sometimes you need to round only one of the numbers. Look at the problem below:

**Estimate 29 × 2. The product is between which numbers?**

     Ⓐ   20 and 70

     Ⓑ   100 and 150

     Ⓒ   300 and 800

     Ⓓ   1,000 and 1,500

This problem might look difficult, but it's easy if you round the number 29 to the nearest 10. Round the number 29 to 30. Now you're going to estimate the product of 30 × 2. You can probably do that by using mental math. It's 60. Answer choice A is correct.

Let's try one more.

**Estimate 42 × 3. The product is between which numbers?**

     Ⓐ   1,000 and 1,200

     Ⓑ   700 and 900

     Ⓒ   100 and 150

     Ⓓ   20 and 100

Begin by rounding 42 to 40. Then multiply 40 by 3. The product is 120, so answer choice C is correct.

# Practice Questions

## Practice 11: Estimating Multiplication

**DIRECTIONS:**

Choose the best of the answer choices given for each of the following problems. Fill in the circle next to your choice. You may NOT use a calculator.

1.  **Estimate 102 × 2. The product is between which numbers?**

    Ⓐ  20 and 70

    Ⓑ  100 and 150

    ⬤  200 and 400

    Ⓓ  500 and 1,000

    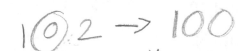

    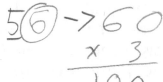

    HINT

    Round 102 to 100.

2.  **Estimate 56 × 3. The product is between which numbers?**

    Ⓐ  1,000 and 1,200

    Ⓑ  500 and 800

    ⬤  100 and 300

    Ⓓ  20 and 100

    HINT

    Round 56 to 60. Then use mental math to estimate the answer.

# Estimating Division

You can also use rounding to estimate division. Note that when you divide one number into another, the number you get is called the **quotient**. Look at this problem:

**Estimate 24 ÷ 5. The quotient is between which numbers?**

    Ⓐ  0 and 5          ⟩2 0

    Ⓑ  5 and 10

    Ⓒ  10 and 20

    Ⓓ  20 and 30

To solve this problem, round 24 to 20. If you divide 5 into 20, the quotient is 4. Answer choice A is correct. Let's try another one.

**Estimate 105 ÷ 10. The quotient is between which numbers?**

    Ⓐ  20 and 30         1 0 0

    Ⓑ  10 and 20

    ⦿  5 and 10

    Ⓓ  0 and 5

To estimate the quotient to this problem, round 105 to 100. Then divide by 10. You can use mental math to figure out how many times 10 goes into 100. (It's 10.) Answer choices B and C both contain 10, but since 105 is greater than 100, the quotient will be greater than 10, so the correct choice is B.

# Practice Questions

## Practice 12: Estimating Division

**DIRECTIONS:**

Choose the best of the answer choices given for each of the following problems. Fill in the circle next to your choice. You may NOT use a calculator.

1. Estimate 43 ÷ 4. The quotient is between which numbers?

   Ⓐ  0 and 5

   Ⓑ  5 and 20

   Ⓒ  20 and 40

   Ⓓ  40 and 60

HINT

Round 43 to 40.

2. Estimate 38 ÷ 2. The quotient is between which numbers?

   Ⓐ  30 and 40

   Ⓑ  10 and 20

   Ⓒ  5 and 10

   Ⓓ  0 and 5

 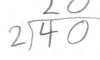

HINT

Round 38 to 40. Then use mental math to divide 2 into 40.

# Practice Questions

## End-of-Chapter Practice Problems

**DIRECTIONS**

Choose the best of the answer choices given for each of the following problems. Fill in the circle next to your choice. You may NOT use a calculator.

1. **Estimate 340 − 190. The difference is between which numbers?**

   Ⓐ 100 and 299

   Ⓑ 300 and 499

   Ⓒ 500 and 699

   Ⓓ 700 and 899

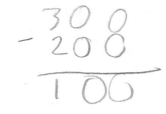

 **HINT**

Begin by rounding the numbers to the nearest hundred. Then subtract them.

2. **Estimate 124 + 65. The sum is between which numbers?**

   Ⓐ 100 and 299

   Ⓑ 300 and 499

   Ⓒ 500 and 599

   Ⓓ 700 and 899

 **HINT**

Round 124 to the nearest hundred. Then round 65 to the nearest ten.

3.  **Estimate 76 ÷ 4. The quotient is between which numbers?**

    Ⓐ   0 and 5

    Ⓑ   5 and 10

    Ⓒ   10 and 30

    Ⓓ   30 and 50

    **HINT**

    Round 76 to 80. Then use mental math to divide 4 into 80.

4.  **Estimate 856 − 91. The difference is between which numbers?**

    Ⓐ   300 and 499

    Ⓑ   500 and 699

    Ⓒ   700 and 999

    Ⓓ   999 and 1,000

    **HINT**

    Round 856 to the nearest hundred. Then round 91 to the nearest ten. Then subtract the numbers by using mental math.

5.  **Estimate 256 + 110. The sum is between which numbers?**

    Ⓐ  300 and 499

    Ⓑ  500 and 699

    Ⓒ  800 and 999

    Ⓓ  999 and 1,000

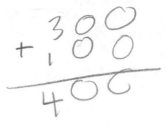

**HINT**

Round each number to the nearest hundred.

6.  **Estimate 24 × 3. The product is between which numbers?**

    Ⓐ  20 and 80

    Ⓑ  80 and 100

    Ⓒ  200 and 400

    Ⓓ  500 and 1,000

**HINT**

Round 24 to 20. Then use mental math to multiply 20 × 3.

# Chapter 4

# All About Lines and Shapes

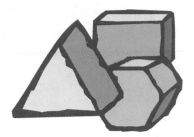

Mathematics is about more than just numbers. It is also about lines and shapes. Questions about lines and shapes might ask how many sides a square has or what type of shape a square is. (A square has four sides and it is a rectangle.) In this chapter, you'll learn about lines and shapes.

## Lines

A **line** is straight. To show that a line goes in two directions, it has arrows at the ends. A line keeps on going. It doesn't have a beginning or an ending. You can see a line below:

A **line segment** is part of a line. It is different from a line, because it has a beginning and an ending. A point is used to show where a line segment begins and ends. This point is called an **endpoint**. Look at the line segment shown below. It has two endpoints.

A **ray** is also part of a line. It's different from a line segment, though. A ray has one endpoint and one arrow. The arrow means that it keeps on going in that direction. The endpoint means that it stops in the other direction. You can see a ray below. Notice that it has one endpoint and one arrow.

Two rays can make an **angle**. Look at the angle below. Each of the rays has an arrow at one end. The point where the rays meet is called the **vertex**. Each ray is called a **side** of an angle.

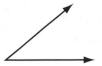

**See if you can name each of the figures below. Write the name of the figure on the line beneath it.**

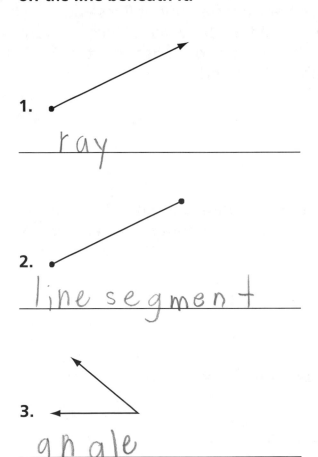

1.

    ray

2.

    line segment

3.

    angle

4.

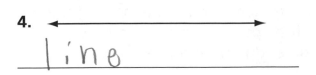

    line

**Now fill in the blank with the correct word.**

5.  **The point that shows where a line segment begins and ends is called an** _end points_ .

6.  **A** _line_ **has two arrows at the ends.**

7.  **Two rays can make an** _angle_ .

8.  **The point where two rays meet is called a** _vertex_ .

9.  **Each ray is called a** _side_ **of an angle.**

Check your answers to these questions with the correct answers below:

1. a ray
2. a line segment
3. an angle
4. a line
5. endpoint
6. line
7. angle
8. vertex
9. side

# Practice Questions

## Practice 13: Lines

**DIRECTIONS:**

Choose the best of the answer choices given for each of the following problems. Fill in the circle next to your choice.

1. Which of these is a line segment?

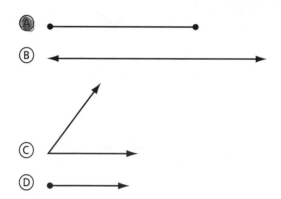

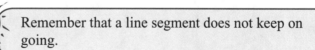

Remember that a line segment does not keep on going.

2.   **What is *A* called in the line segment *AB*?**

*A*               *B*

Ⓐ   vertex

Ⓑ   segment

● endpoint

Ⓓ   side

HINT

If you can't remember what the points in a line segment are called, turn back to the beginning of this chapter.

# Two-Dimensional Shapes

**Two-dimensional** shapes are flat. They have a **length** and a **height**, but they don't have a **width**. The shapes below are two-dimensional. Study the names of these shapes and the number of sides in each shape.

A **triangle** is a figure with three sides. Triangles come in different shapes and sizes. Their sides can be equal, but they don't have to be.

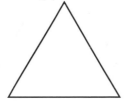 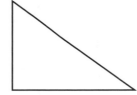

A **rectangle** has four sides and four corners. The sides across from each other have equal lengths. Rectangles can be different sizes, but two pairs of sides will always be equal.

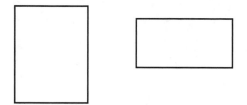

A **square** is a special kind of rectangle that has four equal sides. Squares can be different sizes, but all the sides are always equal.

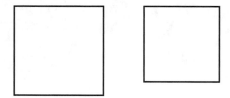

A **pentagon** is a shape with five sides. These sides do not have to be equal.

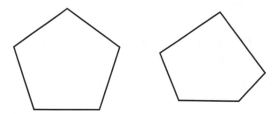

A **hexagon** is a shape with six sides. These sides do not have to be equal.

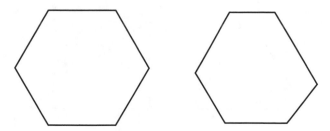

An **octagon** is a shape with eight sides. These sides do not have to be equal.

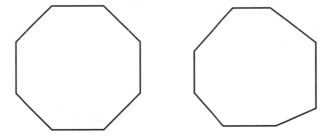

Look at the following two-dimensional shapes. Write what kind of shape each is on the line below it.

**1.**

square

**2.**

rectangle

**3.**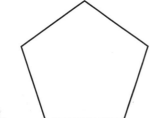

pentagon

**4.**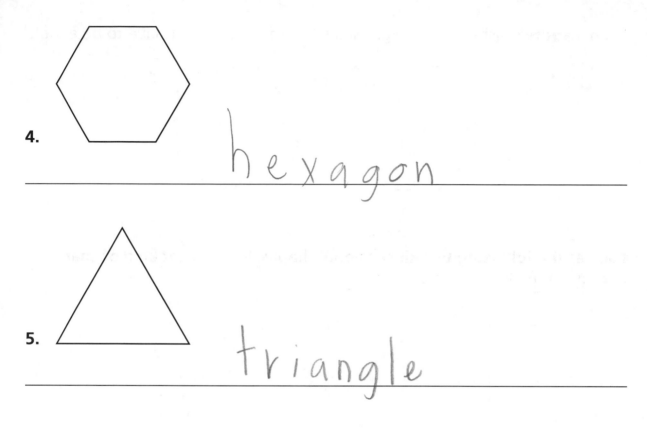

hexagon

**5.**

triangle

Now fill in the blank with the correct word.

6. A hexagon is a shape with six sides, and these sides do not have to be equal.

7. A square has four sides that are the same length.

8. A rectangle has four sides, and two pair of these sides are equal.

9. A triangle has three sides, and these sides do not have to be equal.

10. An _octago_ has eight sides, and these sides do not have to be equal.

11. A _pentagon_ has five sides, and these sides do not have to be equal.

Check your answers to these questions with the correct answers below:

1. square ✓
2. rectangle ✓
3. pentagon ✓
4. hexagon ✓
5. triangle ✓
6. hexagon ✓
7. square ✓
8. rectangle ✓
9. triangle ✓
10. octagon ✓
11. pentagon ✓

# Practice Questions

## Practice 14: Two-Dimensional Shapes

**DIRECTIONS:**

Choose the best of the answer choices given for each of the following problems. Fill in the circle next to your choice.

1.  Which shape below is a hexagon?

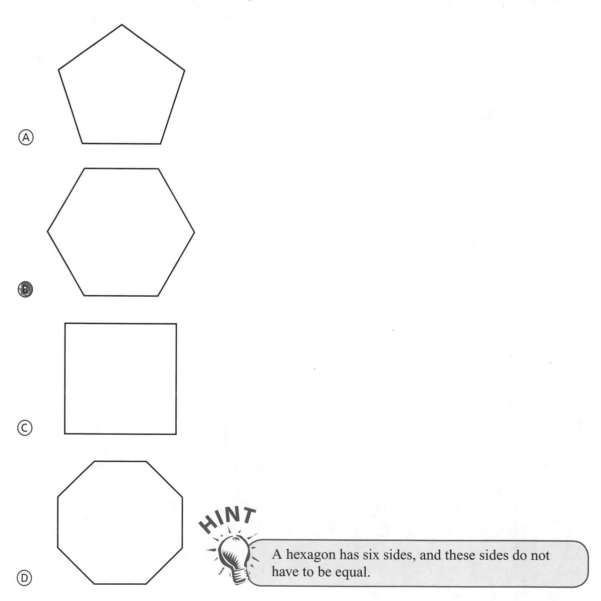

Ⓐ

Ⓑ

Ⓒ

Ⓓ

HINT

A hexagon has six sides, and these sides do not have to be equal.

2. **What shape has eight sides that do not have to be equal?**

   Ⓐ rectangle

   Ⓑ octagon

   Ⓒ square

   Ⓓ circle

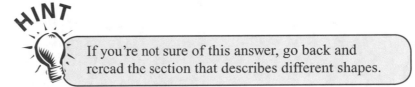

HINT

If you're not sure of this answer, go back and reread the section that describes different shapes.

# Three-Dimensional Shapes

**Three-dimensional** shapes look different from two-dimensional shapes. They have a length, a width, and a height. The six shapes that follow are three-dimensional. Three-dimensional shapes are sometimes called **solids**.

Look at the three-dimensional shape shown below. It is a **cube**. It looks like a square, but it has width. Notice that there are special names for parts of three-dimensional shapes. Each flat part on a three-dimensional shape is called a **face**. The lines in the shape are called **edges**. The edges meet at **corners**.

Using the picture at right, let's review the features of a cube:

- Has flat sides called faces.

- Has edges to connect the faces.

- Has corners that connect the edges.

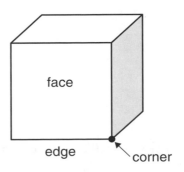

A **cube** looks like a block. Each face on the cube is shaped like a square.

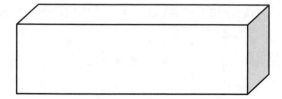

This is a **rectangular prism**. It looks a lot like a box.

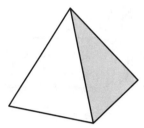

This is a **triangular prism**. It is also called a pyramid. The base of a pyramid is often a square.

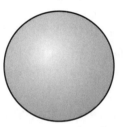

A **sphere** (above) has no faces. It looks like a ball.

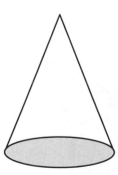

A **cone** looks just like an ice-cream cone. It only has one face. This face is a circle.

A **cylinder** has a top face and a bottom face. Both of these faces are circles. A can is an example of a cylinder.

**Look at each of the three-dimensional shapes below. Write what kind of shape it is on the line below it.**

1.

_____Square_____

2.

_____cone_____

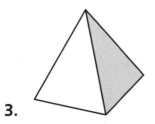

3.

_____pyramid_____

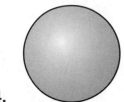

4. <u>sphere</u>

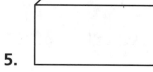

5. <u>rectangular prisum</u>

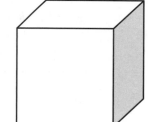

6.

<u>cube</u>

**Now fill in the blank with the correct word.**

7.  **The flat part of a three-dimensional shape is called the** <u>face</u> .

8.  **The edges of a three-dimensional shape meet at the** <u>corners</u> .

9.  **A** <u>sphere</u> **has no faces.**

10. A _cone_ looks like an ice-cream cone.

11. The base of a _____ is often a square.

12. A _____ looks like a box.


Check your answers to these questions with the correct answers below:

1. square

2. cone

3. pyramid, or triangular prism

4. sphere

5. rectangular prism

6. cube

7. face

8. corners

9. sphere

10. cone

11. triangular prism or pyramid

12. rectangular prism

# Practice Questions

## Practice 15: Three-Dimensional Shapes

**DIRECTIONS:**

Choose the best of the answer choices given for each of the following problems. Fill in the circle next to your choice.

1.  Which shape below is a cube?

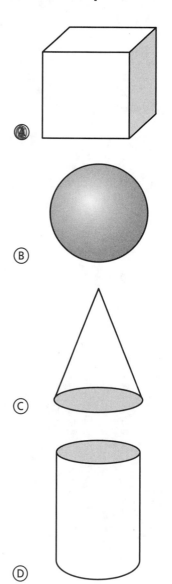

Ⓐ

Ⓑ

Ⓒ

Ⓓ

HINT

Remember that a cube looks like a block.

2.  **Which shape does NOT have a face?**

&#9398; triangular prism

&#9399; cone

&#9400; cylinder

&#9401; sphere

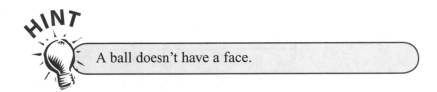

HINT

A ball doesn't have a face.

# Lines of Symmetry

If you cut some shapes in half, the two **halves** will look exactly the same. Shapes such as this are said to have a **line of symmetry**. This line is imaginary and exists only if the two halves of a shape are exactly the same.

Look at the shapes below. Each shape has a line of symmetry. This line is in the center of the shape.

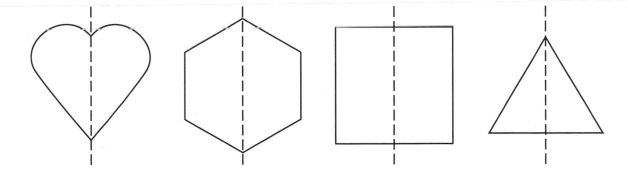

Now look at these shapes. They have a dotted line, but they are not the same on both sides of the line. In fact, these shapes do not have a center, and they do not have a line of symmetry.

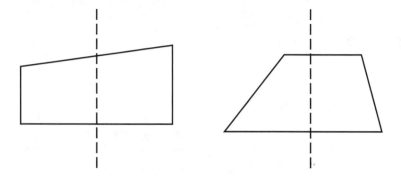

Now you try it.

**Put a check in the box next to each shape that has a line of symmetry.**

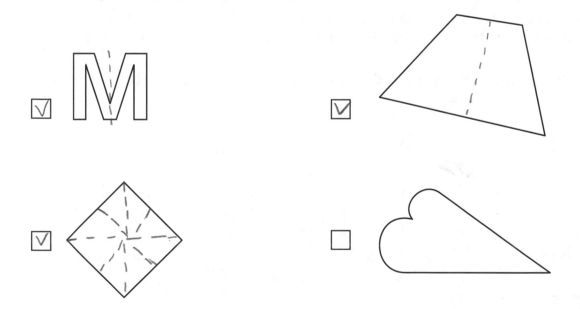

You should have checked only the two shapes on the left.

# Practice Questions

## Practice 16: Lines of Symmetry

**DIRECTIONS:**

Choose the best of the answer choices given for each of the following problems. Fill in the circle next to your choice.

1. Which of these shapes has a line of symmetry?

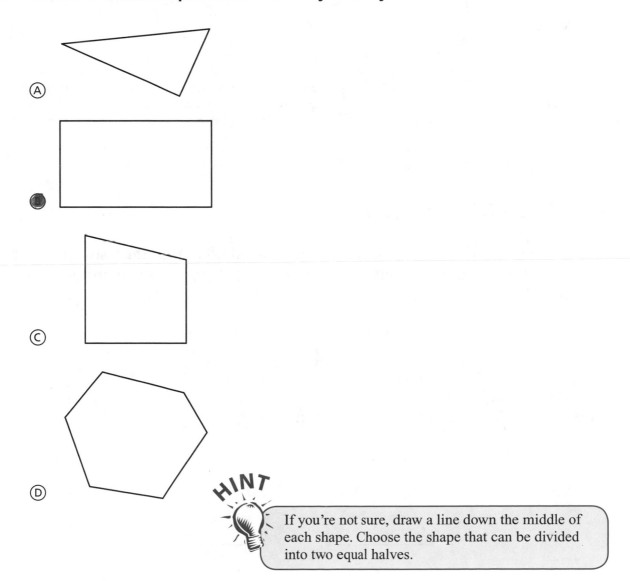

Ⓐ

Ⓑ

Ⓒ

Ⓓ

HINT

If you're not sure, draw a line down the middle of each shape. Choose the shape that can be divided into two equal halves.

2. **Which of these letters has a line of symmetry?**

(A)   **Q**

(B)   **R**

(C)   **W**

(D)   **Z**

Do the same thing here. Choose the letter that you can divide in two equal halves.

# Congruent Shapes

Shapes that are the same size and shape are called **congruent shapes**. Look at the rectangles below. These rectangles are congruent. They are the same shape and size.

Now look at these triangles. They are not congruent.

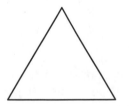 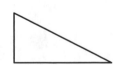

Look at each of the shapes below. Put a check mark in the box next to the shapes that are congruent.

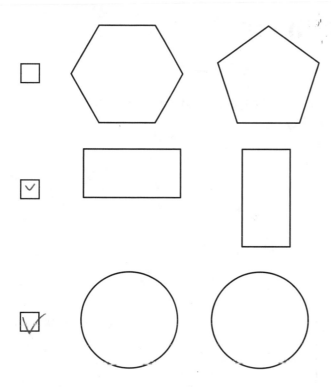

If you checked only the last two pairs, you are correct. The two shapes in the first pair don't even have the same number of sides, so their shapes are different. Even though the rectangles are placed in different directions, they are still considered congruent, because they are the same size and shape.

# Practice Questions

## Practice 17: Congruent Shapes

**DIRECTIONS:**

Choose the best of the answer choices given for each of the following problems. Fill in the circle next to your choice.

1.  Which pair of shapes is congruent?

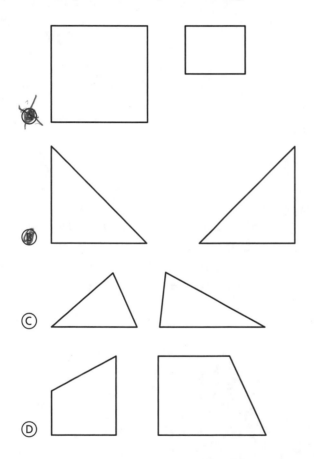

 **HINT**

Choose the pair of shapes that look exactly the same.

2.  **Which pair of shapes is NOT congruent?**

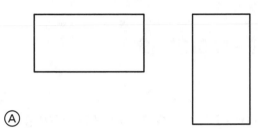

Ⓐ

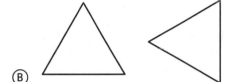

Ⓑ

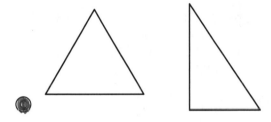

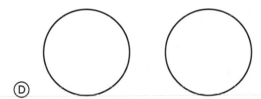

Ⓓ

HINT

This time, you need to choose the shapes that are not exactly the same.

# Practice Questions

## End-of-Chapter Practice Problems

**DIRECTIONS:**

Choose the best of the answer choices given for each of the following problems. Fill in the circle next to your choice.

1.  Which shape is congruent with the shape below?

Ⓐ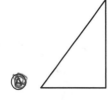

Ⓑ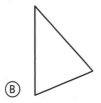

Ⓒ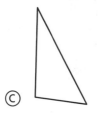

Ⓓ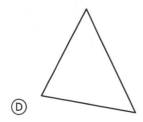

Choose the triangle that is exactly like the triangle above.

2. **Which letter below has a line of symmetry?**

Ⓐ **A**

Ⓑ **D**

Ⓒ **F**

Ⓓ **G**

 If you're not sure, draw a line through each letter.

3.   **Which shape below is a triangular prism?**

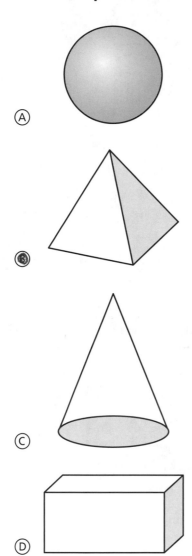

Ⓐ

Ⓑ

Ⓒ

Ⓓ

If you're sure what a triangular prism looks like, turn back to the chapter.

4. **What are the lines below called?**

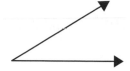

Ⓐ a ray

Ⓑ a line segment

Ⓒ an angle

Ⓓ a line

HINT

These lines are two rays. Do you remember what two rays together are called?

5. **Which shape has three sides that do not have to be equal?**

Ⓐ octagon

Ⓑ pentagon

Ⓒ square

Ⓓ triangle

HINT

Only one of these shapes has only three sides.

6. **Which shape below is a rectangular prism?**

Ⓐ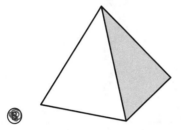

Ⓑ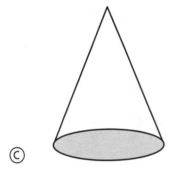

Ⓒ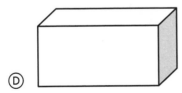

Ⓓ

 A rectangular prism looks like a box.

7. **Which shape below is a pentagon?**

Ⓐ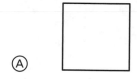

Ⓑ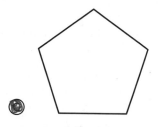

Ⓒ

Ⓓ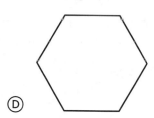

 A pentagon has five sides.

8. **Look at the figures below.**

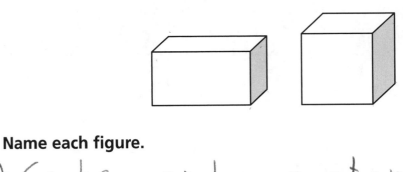

**Name each figure.**

A Cube and a rectangle prisum

• **How many faces does each figure have?**

Each figure has 6 faces

• **Write one way the figures are the same.**

They Both have 8 cormers

• **Write one way the figures are different.**

The yrectangler prim has two eaqul parts and the cud has l

HINT

Count the number of faces. These figures are not congruent. How does that make them different?

# Chapter 5

# More About Shapes

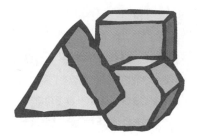

In the last chapter of this book, you learned a lot about lines and shapes. You learned that a line keeps on going in both directions, and this is shown by an arrow on both ends. You also learned that a line segment has endpoints on both ends and that two rays can form an angle. You learned that shapes can be two- or three-dimensional. You learned that there are names for different parts of a three-dimensional shape, such as *vertex*, *edge*, *face*, and *side*.

This chapter gives you more information about shapes. There are three very basic ways you can move a shape: a slide, a flip, and a turn. You'll learn about each of these in this chapter.

A **coordinate grid** plays a very important part in lines and shapes. A coordinate grid looks like a lot of small squares, with a line along the bottom and a line on the left going up to the top of the grid. You can count places along the bottom and side of the grid. You'll learn how to do that in this chapter.

## Moving Shapes

A shape can be moved in three basic ways: a slide, a flip, and a turn. Look at the shape below:

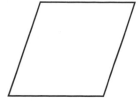

## Slide

If you **slide** the figure above, you move it in one direction. It goes from one place to another without turning. The shape looks as if it is has actually slid. You can slide a shape in any direction. As long as you don't turn it, this move is called a slide. Here are some ways you can slide a shape:

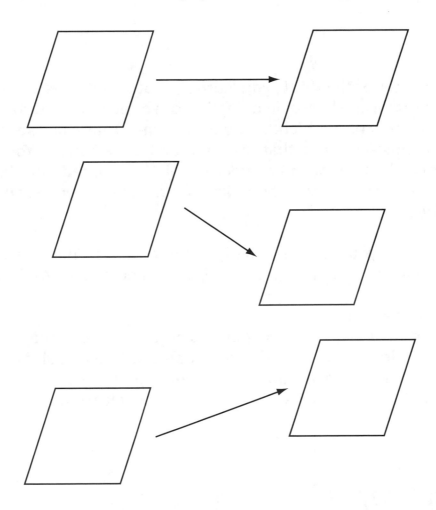

## Flip

A flip is different from a slide. A **flip** takes place when a shape is turned upside-down. Sometimes the shape is flipped across a line, but not always. After a shape is flipped, it is upside-down and facing the opposite direction. It looks as if it is a reflection. This is why a flip is sometimes called a **reflection**. Look at the shape below:

Sometimes the flip is up, or it may be vertical (left or right), but it still looks exactly like a reflection in a mirror.

## Turn

When you **turn** a shape, you move it so it looks as if it is tipping over or lying on its side. Look at the letter below to see how it is turned.

You can also turn a letter like this:

# Practice Questions

## Practice 18: Moving Shapes

**DIRECTIONS:**

Choose the best of the answer choices given for each of the following problems. Fill in the circle next to your choice.

1. Which picture shows only a slide?

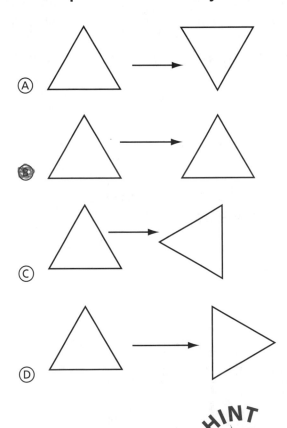

Ⓐ

Ⓑ

Ⓒ

Ⓓ

**HINT**

Remember that a slide doesn't flip. It also doesn't turn.

2.  **Which picture shows a flip?**

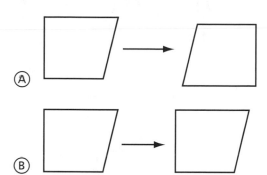

(A)

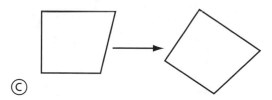

(B)

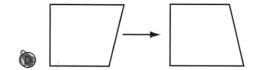

(C)

(D)

HINT

A flip looks like a reflection.

3. **Which picture shows a turn?**

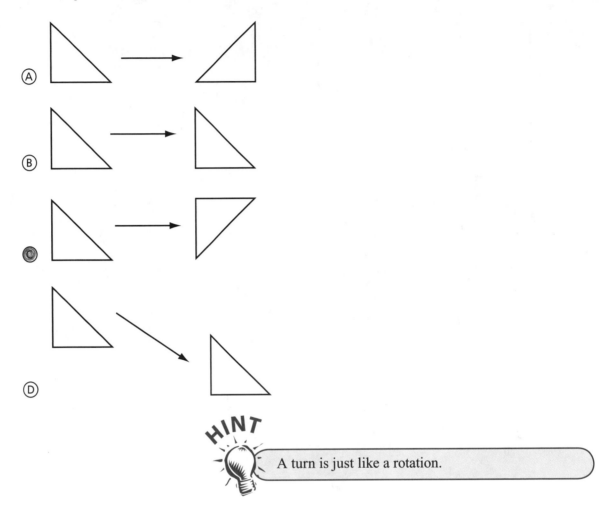

Ⓐ

Ⓑ

Ⓒ

Ⓓ

HINT

A turn is just like a rotation.

# Coordinate Grids

A coordinate grid looks like an array of identical squares. It has two **axes**, or lines. The **x-axis** runs **horizontally** across the grid from left to right, and the **y-axis** runs **vertically** along the grid from the bottom to the top. Each axis has an arrow at the end to show that it keeps on going. Look at the x- and y-axes on this grid. (Note that "**axes**" is the plural of "axis.") Notice that there are numbers on both the x- and y-axes.

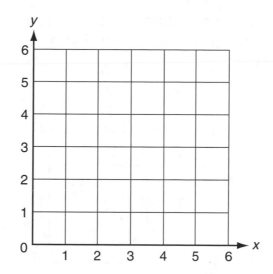

The places on the grid where the grid lines cross are called **points**. Each point has an address, just like your house or apartment has an address. When you identify a point, you count across from **zero** on the *x*-axis and then count up the *y*-axis until you hit that point. This is the point's address, which is called its **coordinates**. Look at the point on this coordinate grid:

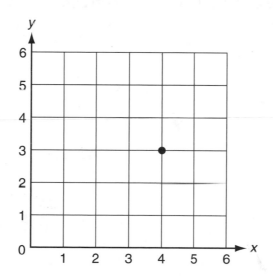

Its coordinates are (4, 3), which is in the form (*x*, *y*). Coordinates always have the horizontal (*x*) value first. The coordinates of this point are at *x* = 4 and *y* = 3, so its address is (4, 3).

Now you try it. What are the coordinates for points *A* and *B* on the grid on the next page? Remember to begin counting on the *x*-axis. This is the number that comes first.

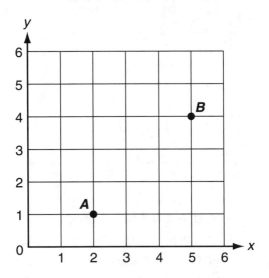

If you determined that the coordinates of point *A* are (2, 1) and the coordinates of point *B* are (5, 4), you are correct.

# Practice Questions

## Practice 19: Coordinate Grids

**DIRECTIONS:**

Choose the best of the answer choices given for each of the following problems. Fill in the circle next to your choice.

1. Which ordered pair shows the location of Katie's school?

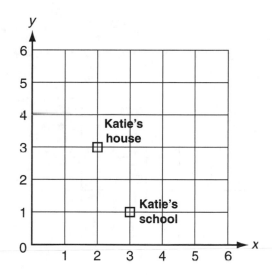

Ⓐ  (0, 3)

Ⓑ  (1, 3)

Ⓒ  (3, 1)

Ⓓ  (3, 3)

**HINT**

Begin by finding the school on the grid. Count across on the *x*-axis first. Then count up on the *y*-axis. Remember that the *x* value goes first.

2.  **Which ordered pair shows the location of Katie's house?**

    Ⓐ  (2, 2)

    Ⓑ  (2, 3)

    Ⓒ  (3, 1)

    Ⓓ  (3, 2)

Find Katie's house on the grid. Count over on the *x*-axis. Then count up on the *y*-axis.

3.  **Which ordered pair shows the location of Point *A*?**

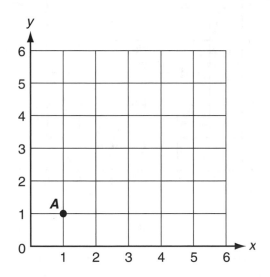

    Ⓐ  (0, 0)

    Ⓑ  (0, 1)

    Ⓒ  (1, 0)

    Ⓓ  (1, 1)

Find Point *A* on the grid. Count over on the *x*-axis. Then count up on the *y*-axis.

# Practice Questions

## End-of-Chapter Practice Problems

**DIRECTIONS:**

Choose the best of the answer choices given for each of the following problems. Fill in the circle next to your choice.

1.  **Which figure shows only a slide?**

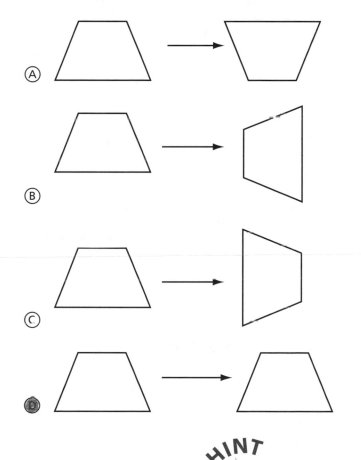

Ⓐ

Ⓑ

Ⓒ

Ⓓ

HINT

Remember that a slide just slides. It doesn't turn.

2. **Which ordered pair shows the location of Marty's house?**

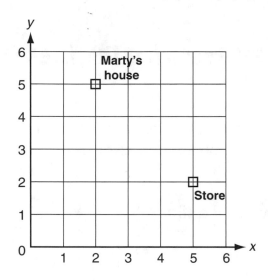

Ⓐ (1, 5)

Ⓑ (2, 4)

● (2, 5)

Ⓓ (3, 5)

Find Marty's house. Then count along the *x*-axis. Then count up along the *y*-axis.

3. **Which ordered pair shows the location of the store?**

Ⓐ (2, 4)

Ⓑ (2, 5)

Ⓒ (5, 1)

● (5, 2)

Now find the store. Be sure to put the *x*-coordinate first.

4.   **What are the coordinates of Point *A*? Explain your answer.** _It's_
_(1,4) I figured it out by going_
_left then up_

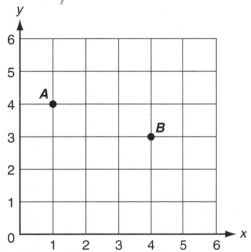

HINT

You have to write out your answer to this question. First find Point A and its coordinates. Then explain in a sentence or ~~two~~ tell how you figured this out.

5.   **Draw a flip of the shape shown below.**

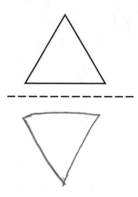

Remember that a flip is like a reflection. The figure you draw should look like an upside-down version of the triangle that is shown.

# Chapter 6

# Measuring

You've probably heard people talk about how tall they are. And you have probably seen a gallon of milk. You may have also seen road signs telling how many miles to the closest town. All of these things tell about measurements.

We use measurements every day to give information about the world around us. Think of something else we measure. Write your idea on the line below.

_____

In this chapter, you'll learn about the different ways in which things can be measured.

## Units of Measurement

You can measure something by using different kinds of units, such as inches or miles, or perhaps pounds or tons. These units are called **units of measurement**.

## Length

**Length** refers to how long something is. You can measure small objects by using inches. An **inch** is a unit of measurement. A **fraction of an inch** is a part of an inch. Have you ever used a **ruler** for measuring length? If you have, you have probably seen inches marked off on a ruler. The lines that mark off inches are usually longer than the other lines on a ruler. The smaller lines are used for fractions of inches. Look at the line segment below:

Use a ruler to measure the line and write your answer below:

_____1 inch_____

If you wrote 1 inch, you are correct.

Most rulers measure up to 12 inches. Twelve inches equals one **foot**. A one-foot ruler is good to measure things like line segments. It is also good to measure anything that is a few inches long.

But what do you use to measure things that are longer than 12 inches? You can use **feet** to do this. Do you know how tall you are? Your height is often measured in feet. Feet are also used to measure short distances. Longer rulers can have a few feet. A **measuring tape** has many feet.

You can use yards to measure things that are longer than a few feet. There are three feet in a yard. People sometimes measure short **distances** by using yards. Have you ever watched a football game? If you have, you might know that the distance the players run across the field is measured in yards. A football field is 100 yards long, and the middle line on the field is called the 50-yard line because it is 50 yards from either end.

Very large distances of thousands of feet are measured in **miles**. There are 5,280 feet in every mile. Imagine that your grandmother lives five miles away. It is easier to say that she lives five miles away than to say she lives 26,400 feet away! Complete the exercise below about measurement.

**Fill in the blank with the correct unit of measurement.**

1.  **The long lines on a ruler are used to measure** _inches_____.

2.  **Very long distances are measured in** _mile_____.

3.  One yard equals three ___*feet*___ .

4.  Twelve inches equals one ___*foot*___ .

If your answers were …

1. inches

2. miles

3. feet

4. foot

… you are correct. If you missed one of more answers, review the beginning of this chapter.

# Metric Units for Length

The metric system for length is based on a **meter** (a little longer that 3 feet). You can measure small objects by using **centimeters** (cm).

This line is one centimeter long. Centimeters are smaller than inches (there are about 2.5 cm in an inch). Can you think of a small object that could be measured in centimeters? You could measure a caterpillar in centimeters. You could also measure a paper clip in centimeters. Sometimes a ruler has inches marked on one side and centimeters marked on the other side.

**Decimeters** are the next largest metric unit of measurement. There are 10 centimeters in every decimeter. Most people use centimeters or meters rather than decimeters for measuring length. There are 100 centimeters in a **meter**. You might use meters to measure distances or even larger objects. People often use meters to measure wrapping paper or cloth.

To measure long distances, you would use **kilometers**. There are 1,000 meters in 1 kilometer. If you wanted to measure the distance to your grandmother's house across town, you would measure it in kilometers. Often races are measured in kilometers. A full marathon is 42.2 kilometers (a little more than 26 miles). A popular race that families run is called a 6K marathon (for 6 kilometers), which is about $3\frac{3}{4}$ miles.

**Complete the following exercises about measurement.**

**Fill in the blank with the correct metric unit of measurement.**

1. A _meter_ is a little longer than three feet.

2. A _centometer_ is the unit used to measure small objects.

3. _kilometer_ are units used to measure very long distances.

4. There are 10 centimeters in a _decimeter_.

If you answered …

1. meter
2. centimeter
3. kilometers
4. decimeter

… you are correct. If you missed one or more answers, review the discussion on metric units of length.

# Practice Questions

## Practice 20: Units of Measurement

**DIRECTIONS:**

Choose the best of the answer choices given for each of the following problems. Fill in the circle next to your choice.

1. **What unit would you use to measure the height your room?**

   Ⓐ centimeters

   Ⓑ feet

   Ⓒ miles

   Ⓓ kilometers

> Think about the distance from your bedroom floor to the ceiling. Is it very small or very large? It is probably somewhere in the middle. Choose the answer that is somewhere in the middle.

2. **What unit would you use to measure the width of a penny?**

   Ⓐ centimeters

   Ⓑ yards

   Ⓒ meters

   Ⓓ miles

> A penny is very small. Make sure you pick a unit of measurement that can measure something so small!

# Weight

When you go to the doctor, you get weighed on a scale. A person's weight is usually measured in **pounds**.

To measure smaller items, we use **ounces**. Think of a regular slice of bread. It weighs about one ounce. There are 16 ounces in every pound. That means that 16 slices of bread equal 1 pound.

**Tons** are used to measure very large things. There are 2,000 pounds in 1 ton. Think of a car. A regular car weighs about $1\frac{1}{2}$ tons! That's really heavy!

**Complete the exercises below about weight.**

1.  Your weight is measured in <u>*pounds*</u>.

2.  A slice of bread weighs about one <u>*ounce*</u>.

3.  There are 2,000 pounds in a <u>*ton*</u>.

If you answered …

1. pounds

2. ounce

3. ton

… you are correct. If you missed one or more of these answers, review the discussion above on weight.

# Metric Units for Weight

Just like length, weight can also be measured by using metric units. **Grams** are used to tell the weight of very tiny objects. A paper clip weighs about one gram. That's very light!

**Kilograms** are used to measure bigger things. There are 1,000 grams in every kilogram. One kilogram is a little more than two pounds.

What do you think you might use to measure a desk lamp? Grams? No, that's much too small. Ounces? Still a little too small. Tons? No, that's much too big! How about pounds? A regular desk lamp might weigh a few pounds. You might also use kilograms to measure a desk lamp. Because two pounds is roughly equal to one kilogram, either of these units could be used.

**Complete this exercise about measuring weight by using metric units.**

1. _____kilograms_____ are used to weigh very large objects.

2. There are 1,000 grams in every _____kilogram_____.

3. _____gram_____ are used to weigh things that are very small.

If you answered …

1. Kilograms
2. kilogram
3. Grams

… you are correct. If you missed one or more of these answers, review the discussion above on metric units for weight.

# Practice Questions

## Practice 21: Weight

**DIRECTIONS:**

Choose the best of the answer choices given for each of the following problems. Fill in the circle next to your choice.

1.  **What unit of measurement might you use to measure a house?**

   Ⓐ grams

   Ⓑ ounces

   Ⓒ kilograms

   Ⓓ tons

HINT

A house is really big! You need a large unit of measure to measure it.

2. **A scale is used to weigh an object. The scale reads 5 grams. What object is most likely being weighed?**

   Ⓐ a dog

   Ⓑ a nickel

   Ⓒ a truck

   Ⓓ a book

HINT

Remember, grams measure very tiny objects. Look at the answer choices and pick the smallest object.

# Capacity

The word **capacity** means how much a container can hold. There are different ways to measure capacity.

Do you like to eat cereal with a teaspoon or a tablespoon? A **teaspoon** is a small spoon. A tablespoon is a larger spoon. There are three teaspoons in every **tablespoon**.

An ordinary **cup** holds about 16 tablespoons of liquid. The next largest unit of measurement is a **pint**. There are two cups in every pint. The milk and juice cartons that come with most school lunches are measured in pints.

A **quart** holds about two pints of liquid. Sometimes a container of milk that you buy at a grocery store will come in a quart size.

Larger amounts of liquids, such as water, are usually measured in **gallons**. You can also buy a gallon of milk, which holds about four quarts.

**Complete this exercise about measuring capacity.**

1. A _tabel spoon_ is bigger than a teaspoon.

2. A _gallon_ holds about 16 tablespoons of liquid.

3. Large amounts of liquid are measured in _cup_.

4. A _quart_ holds about two pints of liquid.

If you answered ...

1. tablespoon
2. cup
3. gallons
4. quart

... you are correct. If you missed one or more of these answers, review the discussion on capacity.

# Practice Questions

## Practice 22: Capacity

**DIRECTIONS:**

**Choose the best of the answer choices given for each of the following problems. Fill in the circle next to your choice.**

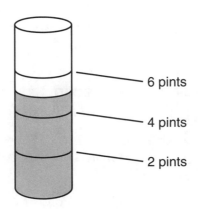

6 pints

4 pints

2 pints

**1.** **Look at the container. About how much liquid is in this container?**

(A) 6 pints

(B) 5 pints

(C) 4$\frac{1}{2}$ pints

(D) 4 pints

 Carefully see where the shaded area ends. Between what two numbers does the shaded area end?

**2.** **Which would you use to measure the amount of water in a swimming pool?**

(A) cups

(B) pints

(C) quarts

(D) gallons

 A swimming pool is pretty big! Remember that you will need a larger unit to measure the amount of water in a pool.

# Perimeter

The **perimeter** of something is the **sum** of the lengths of all of the sides. Perimeter measures the distance around an object. To find the perimeter of most objects, you need to add the **lengths** of all the sides together.

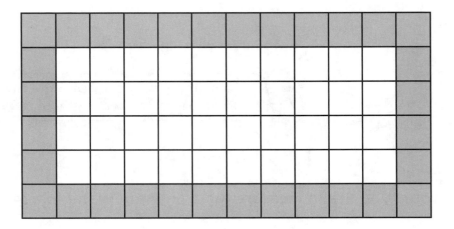

There are 12 unit edges on each of the two long sides of the pool. When you add them together, you get 24. There are 6 unit edges that run along each of the two shorter sides of the pool. By adding those two together, you get 12. Now you need to add the **sum of the lengths** of the two longer sides with the sum of the lengths of the two shorter sides to get the perimeter: 24 + 12 = 36. The perimeter of this pool is 36 units.

Now, let's take a look at another object to find its perimeter. Suppose you have measured all of the sides of a triangle like the one below:

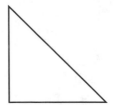

Using your ruler, you find that one side of the triangle measures 1 inches. Another side measures 1 inches. The last side measures 1.5 inches.

To find the perimeter, you need to add all of these inches together like you did with the blocks around the pool.

# Area

**Area** measures the amount of space covered by an object. You could measure the area of objects such as a rug.

You can figure out the area of an object by counting the units needed to cover it.

Look at the square below:

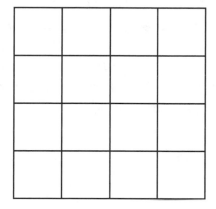

Count all of the blocks that cover the square. There are 16 blocks. So the amount of space (area) that this square takes up is equal to 16 blocks.

Let's try another example. Take a look at the shaded triangle in the square:

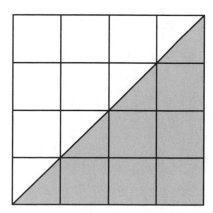

You already know that the square has an area of 16 blocks. What part of the square does the triangle cover?

Count the number of blocks that the triangle covers. Parts of the triangle cover only half of a block. When you have two halves, add them together to make one whole block.

When you are finished, you should come up with the number 8. The triangle covers 6 whole blocks, and it also covers 4 half blocks. When you add each of the halves together, you get 2 whole blocks. 2 + 6 = 8.

You can also figure out this problem by using fractions.

There is another way to figure out the area of the triangle. By looking at the shaded blocks, you can see that the triangle covers half of the square. You know that the square covers an area of 16 blocks. Can you figure out what half of 16 is? You may be able to use mental math to figure this out. Otherwise, use the fact that taking half of something means the same as dividing by the number 2. Half of 16 is 8.

# Practice Questions

## Practice 23: Perimeter and Area

**DIRECTIONS:**

**Choose the best of the answer choices given for each of the following problems. Fill in the circle next to your choice.**

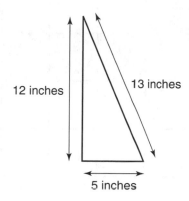

12 inches   13 inches

5 inches

1.  **What is the perimeter of the triangle shown above (figure not drawn to scale)?**

    Ⓐ  18 inches

    Ⓑ  20 inches

    Ⓒ  25 inches

    Ⓓ  30 inches

Remember, the sides have already been measured for you. All you need to do is add them all together.

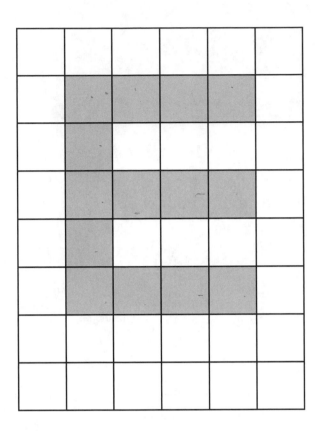

2.  **What area do the shaded blocks in the figure above cover?**

    (A)  12

    (B)  14

    (C)  16

    (D)  20

Remember, when you are solving an area problem, you want to see how much space an object covers. Count all of the shaded blocks to find the area.

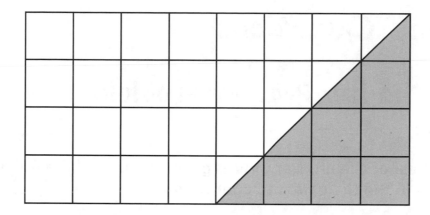

3.  **What is the area of the shaded triangle?**

(A)  9

(B)  15

(C)  16

(D)  8

Remember, if the triangle takes up half of a block, you can add to halves to get one whole block.

# Practice Questions

## End-of-Chapter Practice Problems

**DIRECTIONS:**

Choose the best of the answer choices given for each of the following problems. Fill in the circle next to your choice.

1.  **Measure this line segment using a ruler. How long is this line?**

    ●————————————————————————————●

    Ⓐ   $1\frac{1}{2}$ inches

    Ⓑ   $2\frac{1}{4}$ inches

       $3\frac{1}{2}$ inches

    Ⓓ   $4\frac{1}{4}$ inches

HINT

Make sure that the beginning of your ruler lines up with the beginning of the line. This will help you get the correct answer.

2. **Lisa decided to weigh her dog. Using a scale, Lisa found that her dog weighs about 32 pounds. Which metric unit of measurement might Lisa use to weigh her dog?**

    kilograms

   Ⓑ grams

   Ⓒ centimeters

   Ⓓ meters

   **HINT**

   First, think about what we are measuring. Make sure that you choose a unit of measurement that is used to figure out an object's weight. Second, think about which metric unit is closest to a pound. This will help you choose the best answer.

3. **Rich is baking a birthday cake. He is using a pitcher to measure the water he needs.**

   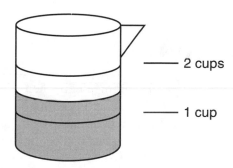

   ——— 2 cups

   ——— 1 cup

   **How much water is in the pitcher?**

   Ⓐ $\frac{1}{2}$ cup

   Ⓑ 1 cup

   Ⓒ $1\frac{1}{2}$ cups

   Ⓓ 2 cups

   **HINT**

   Look at where the shaded area ends. What numbers does it fall between? Carefully look over the choices before selecting an answer.

**4.** **What is the perimeter of this object?**

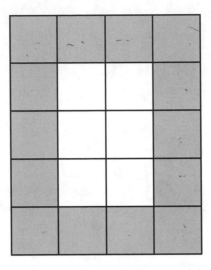

Ⓐ   8 units

Ⓑ   10 units

Ⓒ   14 units

Ⓓ   18 units

 HINT

Remember, when you are figuring out perimeter, you are counting the unit edges that are on each side of the object. Then you need to add all of those unit edges together to find the perimeter.

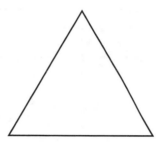

5. Use your ruler to measure each side of the triangle above. What is the perimeter of the triangle?

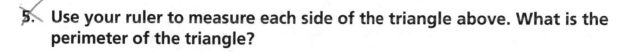

Ⓐ 2 inches

Ⓑ $3\frac{1}{2}$ inches

Ⓒ 4 inches

Ⓓ $4\frac{1}{2}$ inches

HINT

Remember to add all the sides together after you measure them.

6. Your friend Julie lives in another town. What unit of measurement would you use to figure out the distance from your house to Julie's?

Ⓐ miles

Ⓑ yards

Ⓒ feet

Ⓓ inches

HINT

Think about the normal distance between most towns. You would need a large unit of measurement to figure out such a distance.

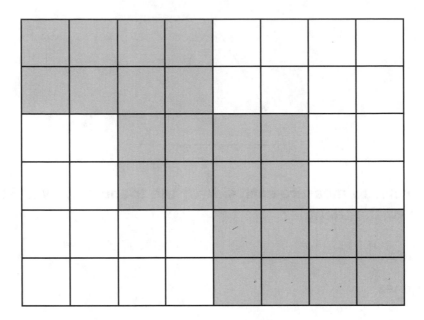

7.  **What area do the shaded blocks in the figure above cover?**

    Ⓐ   12 blocks

    Ⓑ   16 blocks

    Ⓒ   20 blocks

    Ⓓ   24 blocks

 HINT

Remember, when you are solving an area problem,
you want to see how much space an object covers.
Count all of the shaded blocks to find the area.

8.  **Which of the following has the same area as the figure above?**

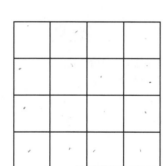

Ⓐ

Ⓒ

Ⓑ

Ⓓ

Count the number of blocks in the first figure. Then count the blocks in each of the figures in the answer choices. Which figure has the same number of blocks as the figure from the question?

# Chapter 7

# Understanding Patterns

In mathematics, patterns are everywhere. If you count by twos—2, 4, 6, 8, and 10—you're using a pattern. If you count by threes or fours, you're also using a pattern. Patterns can also be found in shapes. You'll learn about different patterns in this chapter.

You'll also learn how to use a function machine. A **function** is a kind of pattern. You'll learn about functions and function machines in this chapter.

This chapter will also show you how to find the missing value in a number sentence—for example, what belongs in the box in a sentence such as 2 + 3 = ☐. Multiplication rules such as the **associative** and **commutative properties** are also explained in this chapter.

## Patterns

When you look at a group of numbers, if you can find the pattern, you can tell what number comes next. This is also true with shapes. Look at the table on the next page.

## Mrs. Helms' Bread Baking

| Monday | |
|---|---|
| Tuesday | |
| Wednesday | |
| Thursday | |

= 1 loaf of bread

Do you see the pattern in this table? Mrs. Helms bakes one additional loaf of bread each day of the week. She baked four loaves of bread on Thursday. If this pattern continues, how many loaves of bread will she bake on Friday?

_____

If you said that on Friday Mrs. Helms will bake five loaves of bread, you saw the pattern in the table.

Now look at the pattern below.

If the pattern continues, how many dots will be in the next group?

To find the pattern here, look closely at the dots in the first group and the dots in the second group. Are there more or fewer dots in the second group? There are more. How many more? (If you're not sure, you can count them.) There are two more dots in the second group. And there are two more dots in the third group. The pattern is to add two dots per group. If you add another group, how many dots will be in it? Eight!

# Practice Questions

## Practice 24: Patterns

**Directions for the Open-Ended Questions**

The following questions are **open-ended** questions. Remember to:

Read each question carefully and think about the answer.

Answer all the parts of the question.

Show your work or explain your answer.

You can answer the questions by using words, tables, diagrams, OR pictures. You may use your calculator, ruler, and colored shapes.

1. **You are trying to save money to buy a present for your mother. You record in the chart below the total amount of money you have at the end of each week.**

| Week | 1 | 2 | 3 | 4 | 5 |
|---|---|---|---|---|---|
| Total amount of money saved | $1.50 | $2.00 | $2.50 | $3.00 | |

**If you continue saving money following this pattern, how much money will you have at the end of Week 5? Explain the pattern you used to get your answer.**

_____

_____

_____

_____

This is an open-ended question. You have to write out the answer to this question. How much money is added from Week 1 ($1.50) to Week 2 ($2.00)? From Week 2 ($2.00) to Week 3 ($2.50)? Check to see whether this pattern continues.

**2. Look at the pattern below.**

**A C E G A C E G A**

**What would be the next letter?**

Ⓐ A

Ⓑ C

Ⓒ E

Ⓓ G

HINT

Look for the place where the pattern starts to repeat itself. Then you can figure out which four letters are part of the pattern.

# Function Machines

A **function machine** isn't a real machine. It's an imaginary machine you can use to help you find a pattern. You put a number into the machine. Another number is added to, subtracted from, multiplied by, or divided into this number. Then a new number comes out of the machine and becomes the next number to put into the machine. Look at the function machine below. When 10 is dropped into this machine, it comes out as 8.

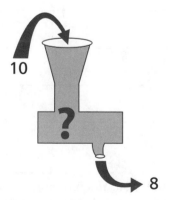

When 8 is dropped in, it comes out as 6.

When 6 is dropped in, it comes out as 4.

**If 4 is dropped into the machine, what number will come out?**

  Ⓐ   4

  Ⓑ   2

  Ⓒ   1

  Ⓓ   0

Begin by looking at the first number put into the function machine: 10. When 10 is put in the machine, it comes out as 8. Is 8 larger or smaller than 10? It's smaller. But by how much? Eight is smaller than 10 by 2.

Now look at the other clues under the function machine. When 8 is dropped in, it comes out as 6. Six is 2 less than 8. The last clue is "When 6 is dropped in, it comes out as 4." The number 4 is also 2 less than 6. So when a number is put into the function machine, it will come out as 2 less.

The question asks you what would happen if you drop the number 4 into the function machine. It will come out as 2 less, so it will come out as 2. Answer choice B is correct.

Let's try another.

When 15 is dropped into this machine, it comes out as 20.

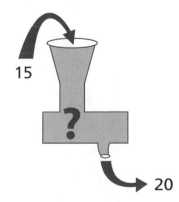

When 20 is dropped in, it comes out as 25.

When 10 is dropped in, it comes out as 15.

**If 25 is dropped into the machine, what number will come out?**

Ⓐ 15

Ⓑ 20

Ⓒ 30

Ⓓ 35

Look for the pattern. Numbers dropped into the function machine increase by 5. If you add 5 to 25, the answer is 30. Answer choice C is correct.

# Practice Questions

## Practice 25: Function Machine

**DIRECTIONS:**

Choose the best of the answer choices given for each of the following problems. Fill in the circle next to your choice.

1. When 12 is dropped into this machine, it comes out as 9.

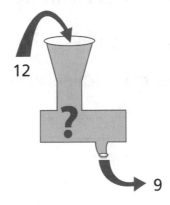

When 10 is dropped in, it comes out as 7.

When 14 is dropped in, it comes out as 11.

If 8 is dropped into the machine, what number will come out?

Ⓐ 4

Ⓑ 5

Ⓒ 6

Ⓓ 7

HINT

Find the difference between 12 and 9, between 10 and 7, and between 14 and 11 to find the pattern for the function machine.

2. When 17 is dropped into this machine, it comes out as 21.

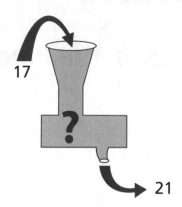

When 15 is dropped in, it comes out as 19.

When 20 is dropped in, it comes out as 24.

When 18 is dropped into the machine, what number will it come out as?

Ⓐ  19

Ⓑ  20

Ⓒ  21

Ⓓ  22

HINT

Find the difference between 17 and 21, between 15 and 19, and between 20 and 24. Do you see the pattern for this function machine?

# Input/Output Tables and T-Charts

You just learned how to use a function machine. The number you put into the machine is called input. The number that comes out of the machine is called **output**. **Input/output** tables are a lot like function machines. Look at the table below:

**Which rule is assigned to the input numbers in order to get the output numbers?**

| Input | Output |
|:-----:|:------:|
| 2 | 5 |
| 3 | 6 |
| 4 | 7 |
| 5 | 8 |

Ⓐ  Add 3

Ⓑ  Subtract 3

Ⓒ  Multiply by 2

Ⓓ  Divide by 2

To answer this question, look closely at the first number in the input column and the first number in the output column. What do you have to do to the number 2 to make it 5? You add 3. Look at the second number. What do you have to do to the number 3 to make it 6? Once again, you add 3. Check the other inputs and outputs to see whether they follow this pattern. Answer choice A is correct.

A **T-chart** is just like an input/output table, but it is set up in a different way. Look at the T-chart below:

| x | y |
|---|---|
| 12 | 8 |
| 10 | 6 |
| 9 | 5 |
| 8 | 4 |

**Which rule is assigned to the x column in order to get the number in the y column?**

&#9398; Add 4

&#9399; Subtract 4

&#9400; Multiply by 2

&#9401; Divide by 2

To answer this question, look closely at the first number in the *x* column. It's 12. What do you have to do to 12 to get 8? You have to subtract 4. If you look at all of the numbers in the *x* column, you'll see that you have to subtract 4 from each to them to get the number in the *y* column. Answer choice B is correct.

# Practice Questions

## Practice 26: Input/Output Tables and T-Charts

**DIRECTIONS:**

Choose the best of the answer choices given for each of the following problems. Fill in the circle next to your choice.

1. Which rule is assigned to the input numbers in the following input/output table to get the output numbers?

| Input | Output |
|:-----:|:------:|
| 2 | 4 |
| 4 | 8 |
| 5 | 10 |
| 7 | 14 |

Ⓐ   Add 4

Ⓑ   Subtract 2

Ⓒ   Multiply by 2

Ⓓ   Divide by 2

Be sure to look at all of the numbers in the input/output table before making a decision.

2. **Which rule is assigned to the numbers in the *x* column to get the numbers in the *y* column?**

| x | y |
|---|---|
| 6 | 4 |
| 5 | 3 |
| 4 | 2 |
| 3 | 1 |

   Ⓐ   Add 2

   Ⓑ   Subtract 2

   Ⓒ   Multiply by 2

   Ⓓ   Divide by 2

**HINT**

Notice that the numbers in the *y* column are smaller than those in the *x* column.

# Open Sentences

For **open sentences**, you have to fill in a blank with the correct number. Look at this open sentence:

$$3 + 7 = \square$$

You can probably solve this problem by using mental math. You might already know that $3 + 7 = 10$.

Let's try another.

$$18 - \square = 12$$

This one is more difficult, although you may be able to use mental math to solve it. You need to figure out what number subtracted from 18 is 12. You can solve this problem **by rearranging the numbers** in the problem. Look at this example of rearrangement.

Can you see that $18 - \square = 12$ is the same as $18 - 12 = \square$?

Now solve the problem. $18 - 12 = 6$. Substitute the 6 in the original open sentence to make sure you have the correct answer:

$18 - 6 = 12$. That's correct!

Sometimes a letter is used in place of the box, and you have to figure out the value of this letter. Look at this open sentence:

$$n = 12 + 5$$

You can use mental math to find

$$12 + 5 = 17$$

so $n$ is 17.

Let's try one more:

$$14 - x = 10$$

This open sentence is asking "What number ($x$), when subtracted from 14, equals 10?" By mental math, you can get that $x$ is 4.

Or you can also rearrange the open sentence as you did before to get $14 - 10 = x$, and then use mental math to get that $x$ is 4.

Now check your answer by substituting 4 in the original open sentence:

$$14 - 4 = 10$$

It works!

**Now solve each of the following open sentences.**

1.  $5 - 3 = \square$

2.  $4 + \square = 9$

3.  $12 - x = 9$

4.  $8 + 9 = n$

5.  $21 - x = 14$

The correct answers are:

1.  2
2.  5
3.  3
4.  17
5.  7

Did you get them all right? If not, review the section on open sentences.

If an open-sentence question has multiple-choice answers, it is often quicker and easier to just substitute these choices into the open sentence to see which one works. This is just like the step for checking your answer at the end of the previous page.

# Practice Questions

## Practice 27: Open Sentences

**DIRECTIONS:**

Choose the best of the answer choices given for each of the following problems. Fill in the circle next to your choice.

1. **What does the *p* equal in 5 + *p* = 21?**

   Ⓐ 11

   Ⓑ 15

   Ⓒ 16

   Ⓓ 17

The question is actually asking, "What number, when added to 5, gives you 21?" You can solve this by substituting each of the multiple-choice answers until you get the right one.

2. **If 32 − ☐ = 23, what is the value of ☐?**

   Ⓐ 7

   Ⓑ 8

   Ⓒ 9

   Ⓓ 23

This question is asking, "What number, when it is subtracted from 32, equals 23?" You can solve this by substituting each of the multiple-choice answers until you get the right one. Another way to solve this problem is to rearrange it to read 32 − 23 = ☐, and subtract 23 from 32.

3. **What does the *n* equal in 13 + *n* = 24?**

    Ⓐ 10

    Ⓑ 11

    Ⓒ 13

    Ⓓ 15

> **HINT**
>
> This open sentence is actually asking, "What number, when added to 13, equals 24?" You can solve this by substituting each of the multiple-choice answers until you get the right one.

4. **If 98 − 14 = ☐ , then what is the value of ☐?**

    Ⓐ 80

    Ⓑ 82

    Ⓒ 84

    Ⓓ 86

> **HINT**
>
> Subtract 14 from 98.

# Number Sentences

Number sentences are a lot like the open sentences you just read about. Look at this example:

**Jennifer had 32 pencils. She gave some of the pencils to her friend. She now has 20 pencils. Which number sentence could you use to find out how many pencils Jennifer gave to her friend?**

(A) $\Box - 20 = 32$

(B) $20 \times \Box = 32$

(C) $20 + 32 = \Box$

(D) $32 - 20 = \Box$

For this problem, you have to choose the answer choice that you could use to find out how many pencils Jennifer gave away. Answer choice A isn't correct. Subtracting 20 from a number, the number Jennifer ended up with, won't tell you how many pencils she gave away.

Answer choice B isn't correct either. You wouldn't multiply to find out how many pencils she gave away.

You would subtract. Adding 20 and 32 (answer choice C) would give you a large number. This number wouldn't tell you how many pencils Jennifer gave away.

But if you subtract 20 from 32 (or how many Jennifer has left from how many she started with), as in answer choice D, you would find out how many pencils she gave away. Jennifer gave away 12 pencils. Answer choice D is correct.

# Practice Questions

## Practice 28: Number Sentences

**DIRECTIONS:**

Choose the best of the answer choices given for each of the following problems. Fill in the circle next to your choice.

1. Peter has 24 crayons. His mother gives him more crayons. He now has 36 crayons. Which number sentence could you use to find out how many crayons his mother gave him?

    Ⓐ  $24 + 36 = \square$

    Ⓑ  $24 + \square = 36$

    Ⓒ  $24 \times \square = 36$

    Ⓓ  $\square + 26 = 24$

HINT

How many more crayons do you need to go from having 24 to having 36?

**2.** Tara has 68 marbles. She gives 24 marbles to her friend. Which number sentence could you use to find out how many marbles Tara has now?

Ⓐ 68 + 24 = ☐

Ⓑ ☐ × 24 = 68

Ⓒ 68 − 24 = ☐

Ⓓ 68 − ☐ = 24

**HINT**

For this problem, you need to subtract 24 from 68.

# Multiplication Rules

The following are some rules for multiplication.

• You can multiply numbers in any order and get the same answer. This is called the **commutative property** of multiplication.

For example, 7 × 3 = 21 is the same as 3 × 7 = 21.

• You can also multiply numbers in any order when you are multiplying more than two numbers. The idea that you can multiply numbers in any order is called the **associative property** of multiplication.

So (7 × 3) × 2 = 42 is the same as 7 × (3 × 2) = 42. Note that parentheses around numbers mean "do me first." Therefore,

(7 × 3) × 2 means 21 × 2, which equals 42.

7 × (3 × 2) means 7 × 6, which also equals 42.

So the order of multiplication doesn't matter.

- Any number multiplied by 1 is that number. The number 1 is called the **identity element** of multiplication.

$$8 \times 1 = 8$$

$$105 \times 1 = 105$$

- Any number multiplied by 0 is 0.

$$9 \times 0 = 0$$

$$72 \times 0 = 0$$

# Practice Questions

## Practice 29: Multiplication Rules

**DIRECTIONS:**

Choose the best of the answer choices given for each of the following problems. Fill in the circle next to your choice.

1.  If 45 × ☐ = 0, then what is the value of ☐?

Ⓐ 0

Ⓑ 1

Ⓒ 5

Ⓓ 45

HINT

Remember the rule about zero.

2. **Which of the following is the same as 2 × (60 × 4)?**

Ⓐ 2 + (60 × 4)

Ⓑ 4 ÷ (2 × 60)

Ⓒ (2 × 60) × 4

Ⓓ 2 × 2 × (60 × 4)

 **HINT**

Go back and reread the rule about the associative property of multiplication if you don't know the answer to this question.

3. **If 100 × ☐ = 100, then what is the value of ☐?**

Ⓐ 0

Ⓑ 1

Ⓒ $\frac{1}{2}$

Ⓓ 100

 **HINT**

Remember that the number 1 is the identity element for multiplication.

# Practice Questions

## End-of-Chapter Practice Problems

**DIRECTIONS:**

Choose the best of the answer choices given for each of the following problems. Fill in the circle next to your choice.

1. Which rule is assigned to the input numbers in order to get the output numbers?

| Input | Output |
|:-----:|:------:|
| 5 | 1 |
| 8 | 4 |
| 10 | 6 |
| 14 | 10 |

Ⓐ  Add 4

●  Subtract 4

Ⓒ  Divide by 4

Ⓓ  Multiply by 4

HINT

Look closely at the numbers in the input column. They get smaller in the output column. By how much do they get smaller?

2. You are trying to save money for a new basketball. You record the total amount of money you have at the end of each week in the chart below.

| Week | 1 | 2 | 3 | 4 | 5 |
|---|---|---|---|---|---|
| Total amount of money saved | $2.75 | $3.50 | $4.25 | $5.00 | |

If you continue saving money following this pattern, how much money will you have at the end of week 5?

Ⓐ $5.25

Ⓑ $5.50

◉ $5.75

Ⓓ $6.25

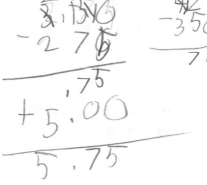

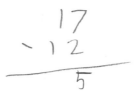

**HINT**

Find the difference between the money in week 1 and the money saved in Week 2. Then find the difference between the money saved in Week 2 and the money saved in Week 3, etc., to find the pattern.

3. 17 − ☐ = 12

Ⓐ 3

Ⓑ 4

◉ 5

Ⓓ 6

**HINT**

What number subtracted from 17 gives 12?

4.   **What does the *n* equal in 7 + *n* = 32?**

ⓐ  20

ⓑ  23

Ⓒ  25

ⓓ  38

HINT

What number added to 7 gives 32?

5.   **Which rule is assigned to the numbers in the *x* column to get the numbers in the *y* column?**

| x | y |
|---|---|
| 12 | 20 |
| 14 | 22 |
| 16 | 24 |
| 18 | 26 |

ⓐ  Multiply by 2

ⓑ  Divide by 2

Ⓒ  Add 8

ⓓ  Add 6

HINT

Look carefully at the numbers in the *x* column and the numbers in the *y* column.

6. **When 20 is dropped into this machine, it comes out as 14.**

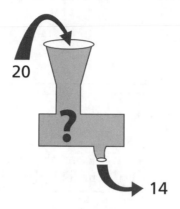

20

?

14

**When 18 is dropped in, it comes out as 12.**

**When 7 is dropped in, it comes out as 1.**

**If 12 is dropped into the machine, what number will come out?**

Ⓐ 10

Ⓑ 8

Ⓒ 6

Ⓓ 4

**HINT**

Find the difference in each pair of numbers when the first is dropped into the function machine and the second comes out.

7. **If 48 − ☐ = 32, what is the value of ☐?**

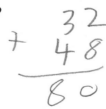

$$\begin{array}{r} 1 \\ 32 \\ + 48 \\ \hline 80 \end{array}$$

Ⓐ 14

Ⓑ 16

Ⓒ 18

Ⓓ 30

**HINT**

What number subtracted from 48 gives 32?

8.   If 68 × ☐ = 0, then what is the value of ☐? Explain your answer.

_____

_____

Remember what happens to a number when it is multiplied by zero.

9.   Renee has 12 bus tokens. Her father gives her some more tokens. She now has 26 tokens. Which number sentence could you use to find out how many tokens her father gave her?

Ⓐ   12 + 26 = ☐

Ⓑ   12 + ☐ = 26

Ⓒ   12 × ☐ = 26

Ⓓ   12 – ☐ = 26

Think about this problem. She now has 26 tokens. What could you add to the number she started with to find out how many tokens her father gave her?

# Chapter 8

# Data Analysis and Probability

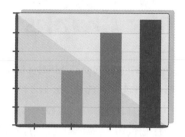

Suppose you would like to find out what sport most of the students in your class like to play. You grab a pencil and paper and ask each student in your class. Then you write down their answers. You use this information to make this decision: Most of the students in your class like soccer!

The information you wrote down is called **data**. People use data in many different ways. The weatherperson on your television gathers data and then makes a prediction about the weather.

Your math teacher might give the students in your class a quiz. If the students do not do well on the quiz, your teacher might decide to spend more time teaching the lesson. The quiz your teacher gave was to gather data, or information, for this decision. In this chapter, you'll learn how to make a decision based on data.

Imagine that you have ten pairs of socks in your sock drawer. Five pairs of these socks are blue, and five pairs are white. You reach into your sock drawer and pull out a pair without looking. Do you think you will pull out a blue pair of socks or a white pair? The likelihood of something happening, like pulling out one color or another, is called **probability**. You'll learn about probability in this chapter, too.

## Using Data

**Data** are often displayed in **graphs** and **tables**. A graph might be used to show how many students attended a school over the past five years. A different kind of graph might be used to show what kind of topping some friends like on a pizza. Let's review some common graphs and tables now.

# Bar Graphs

A **bar graph** uses bars to show data. The bars are usually vertical (up and down). But the bars can also be horizontal (side to side). Often the bars on a bar graph will be printed in different colors, but on the NJ ASK, the bars will be gray. Look at the bar graph shown below:

Number of Points Jamal Scored in First Three Basketball Games

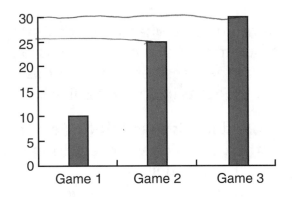

This bar graph shows how many basketball points Jamal scored during his first three basketball games. Each game is listed on the bottom of the graph—Game 1, Game 2, and Game 3. The number of points is listed on the side—0, 5, 10, and so on. Use the bar graph to tell how many points Jamal scored in each game. Game 1 is done for you.

**Game 1**: 10 points

**Game 2**: _25_

**Game 3**: _30_

During which game did Jamal score the most points? _____

If you answered that Jamal scored 25 points in Game 2 and 30 points in Game 3, you are correct. He scored the most points in Game 3.

# Pictographs

A **pictograph** is another kind of graph. In this kind of graph, **pictures** stand for data. A picture often stands for more than one thing. You have to look at a key to see how many things a picture stands for. Look at this pictograph:

## Number of Books Read

| Tyler | 📖 📖 📖 |
|-------|---------|
| Morgan | 📖 📖 📖 📖 |
| Emile | 📖 📖 |
| Ling | 📖 📖 📖 |

Key: 📖 = 2 books

Use the pictograph and the **key** to tell how many books each friend read. The first one is done for you.

Tyler  6 books

Morgan ___8_____

Emile ___4_____

Ling ___6_____

Who read the most books? _Morgan_____

If you answered that Morgan read 8 books, Emile read 4 books, and Ling read 6 books, you are correct. Morgan read the most books.

# Practice Questions

## Practice 30: Bar Graphs

**DIRECTIONS:**

Choose the best of the answer choices given for each of the following problems. Fill in the circle next to your choice.

Time Ruby Spent Doing Homework

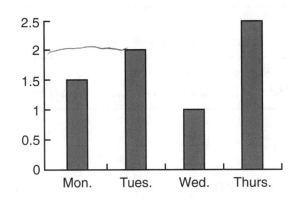

1. **Refer to the bar chart above to find how many hours Ruby studied on Tuesday.**

   Ⓐ  1

   Ⓑ  1.5

   ⬤  2

   Ⓓ  2.5

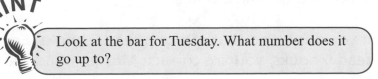

Look at the bar for Tuesday. What number does it go up to?

2.  **According to the bar chart, on which day did Ruby study the most?**

    Ⓐ  Monday

    Ⓑ  Tuesday

    Ⓒ  Wednesday

    Ⓓ  Thursday

HINT

Choose the day with the highest bar.

# Probability

**Probability** is the chance that something will happen. Let's say that you have a bag of 10 jelly beans. You have:

3 red

1 yellow

2 pink

4 green

Imagine that you put your hand in the bag and pull out a jelly bean without looking. What is the chance (probability) that you will pull out a pink jelly bean?

To find out, add up all of the jelly beans. You have 10. Then see how many jelly beans are pink. There are 2. So the probability that you will pull out a pink jelly bean is 2 out of 10.

Let's try another.

Jeremy is about to spin this spinner:

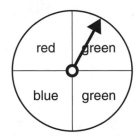

What is the probability that the spinner will land on green?

Begin by determining how many parts are in the spinner. There are 4. Then see how many parts are green. There are 2. So the probability that the spinner will land on a green part is 2 out of 4.

# Practice Questions

## Practice 31: Probability

**DIRECTIONS:**

Choose the best of the answer choices given for each of the following problems. Fill in the circle next to your choice.

1.  Tina has a bag of 10 marbles that contains 2 green marbles, 3 red marbles, 4 black marbles, and 1 white marble. If Tina reached into the bag without looking and picked one marble, what is the probability that she would pick a red marble?

    (A)  1 out of 3

    (B)  3 out of 10

    (C)  7 out of 10

    (D)  3 out of 3

> Remember that there are 10 marbles all together, and 3 of these marbles are red.

2.  The students in Ms. Martino's class must pick a card from a deck. The deck has 10 cards. Three cards have a star on them. Two cards have a heart on them. And five cards have a diamond on them. What is the probability that the first student will pick a card with a diamond?

    (A)  1 out of 5

    (B)  2 out of 10

    (C)  5 out of 10

    (D)  3 out of 10

> There are 10 cards in all. Five of these cards have a diamond on them.

# Practice Questions

## End-of-Chapter Practice

**DIRECTIONS:**

Choose the best of the answer choices given for each of the following problems. Fill in the circle next to your choice.

1. Mr. Renold's class kept track of how many classroom chores they did during the month of October.

| Chris | ☆☆☆☆☆ |
| Eric | ☆☆☆☆ |
| Melanie | ☆☆☆☆☆☆ |
| Karen | ☆☆☆ |

Key: ☆ = 3 chores

**How many chores did Melanie do in October?**

Ⓐ 3

Ⓑ 6

Ⓒ 12

Ⓓ 18

 HINT

Remember to look at the key before choosing an answer.

2.  In her sock drawer, Megan has 3 pairs of white socks, 2 pairs of blue socks, 1 pair of yellow socks, and 3 pairs of tan socks. If she reaches into the drawer without looking, what is the probability that she will pull out a pair of blue socks?

    Ⓐ  3 out of 9

    Ⓑ  1 out of 2

    Ⓒ  2 out of 9

    Ⓓ  1 out of 3

 HINT

Add up the number of pairs of socks in Megan's drawer.

3.  Daryl is going to spin the spinner shown below. What is the probability that the spinner will land on blue?

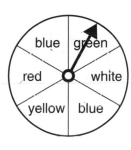

    Ⓐ  1 out of 6

    Ⓑ  1 out of 6

    Ⓒ  2 out of 6

    Ⓓ  2 out of 8

 HINT

Count the total number of sections on the spinner. Then count the number of blue sections.

4.  **The graph below shows how long it took the members of a track team to run a mile. Which girl ran the fastest?**

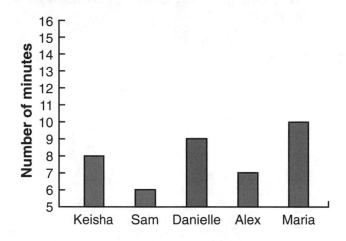

Ⓐ  Keisha

Ⓑ  Sam

Ⓒ  Danielle

Ⓓ  Alex

The fastest runner takes the least amount of time.

# Chapter 9

# More About Analyzing Data

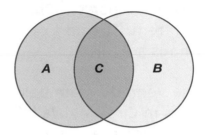

In the last chapter, Chapter 8, you learned how to analyze data in bar graphs and pictographs. You learned about tables, too. These graphs and tables show data.

Data can be shown in other ways, too. Venn and tree diagrams can be used to show data. You'll learn about these in this chapter.

You'll also learn about combinations in this chapter. Suppose you go to an ice cream stand. You learn that you can have your ice cream in either a sugar cone or a waffle cone. And you can choose from chocolate, vanilla, or strawberry ice cream. How many different combinations of cone and ice cream are there? You'll learn how to find the answer to this question in this chapter.

## Venn Diagrams

A **Venn diagram** is used to show how things are alike and how they are different. It has **overlapping circles**. The diagram below is an example of a Venn diagram for two things.

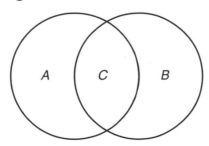

The outer parts of the circles—parts *A* and *B*—show how the two things are different. The part of the circles that overlap—part *C*—shows how the two things are alike.

The Venn diagram below compares dogs and cats. We'll list things about dogs in Circle A. We'll list things about cats in Circle B. The things that dogs and cats have in common go in the part of the circles that overlaps.

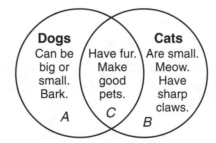

If you look at this Venn diagram, you can see that dogs and cats are alike because they both have fur and they both make good pets. Dogs are different from cats because they can be different sizes and they bark. Cats are different from dogs because they have sharp claws, meow, and are mostly small.

Now try to make your own Venn diagram. Compare yourself with your best friend. Put things about yourself in Circle *A*. Put things about your friend in Circle *B*. Put some ways that you are alike in part *C*.

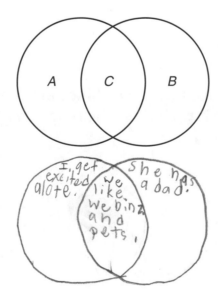

# Tree Diagrams

A **tree diagram** shows the **order** in which something happens. You can tell from a tree diagram what will happen next. Look at this phone tree:

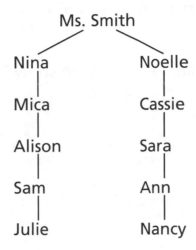

When a girls' basketball practice is cancelled, Ms. Smith, the coach, calls Nina and Noelle. Then Nina and Noelle each call the player listed directly under her name. This continues until every student is told.

Which student will Ann call?

To answer this question, find Ann's name on the tree. Ann will call the person beneath her name. If you look at the tree, you can see that Ann will call Nancy.

# Practice 32: Venn Diagrams and Tree Diagrams

**DIRECTIONS:**

Choose the best of the answer choices given for each of the following problems. Fill in the circle next to your choice.

1. Casey used the Venn diagram below to show how she and her twin brother, Ray, are alike and different.

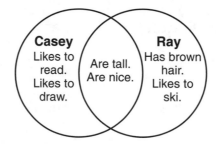

**What can Casey conclude from her Venn diagram?**

Ⓐ Both Casey and Ray like to read.

Ⓑ Both Casey and Ray have brown hair.

Ⓒ Both Casey and Ray like to draw.

Ⓓ Both Casey and Ray are tall.

Remember that the ways in which Casey and Ray are alike are listed in the part where the circles overlap.

2. **When the chess club is planning an activity, Brenda calls Kathy and Rick. Then Kathy and Rick call the students directly under their names, who then call the students listed under their names.**

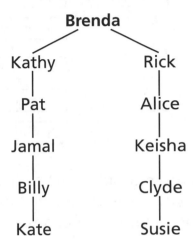

**Which student does Billy call?**

Ⓐ Jamal

Ⓑ Clyde

Ⓒ Kate

Ⓓ Susie

HINT

Find the name that is listed under Billy.

# Combinations

You can make a graph that looks like a tree diagram to find out how many **combinations** of something you have. Remember the combinations of ice cream cones and ice cream you read about in the beginning of this chapter? You had a choice of a sugar cone or a waffle cone. You also had a choice of chocolate, vanilla, or strawberry ice cream. To find out how many combinations of cones and ice cream flavors you have, you can draw a diagram like this:

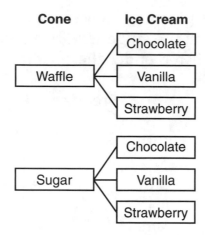

You have to put the ice cream choices next to each kind of cone. To find out how many combinations you have, count the lines. Did you count six lines? There are six different combinations of cones and ice cream.

Let's try another one.

**Jamie has 3 T-shirts: a blue one, a purple one, and a white one. He also has 2 pairs of pants: a gray pair and a brown pair. If an outfit consists of one T-shirt and one pair of pants, how many different outfits can Jamie make?**

In the tree diagram below, all of the different ways to combine the clothes are listed. Just count each possible outfit to figure out the answer:

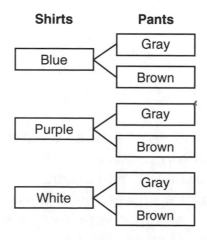

How many different outfits can Jamie make? Remember to count the lines. If you said *six*, you are correct! Now try some questions like this on your own.

# Practice Questions

## Practice 33: Combinations

**DIRECTIONS:**

Choose the best of the answer choices given for each of the following problems. Fill in the circle next to your choice.

1.  Ty is choosing what to order from a menu. He cannot decide whether he wants a chicken sandwich, fish sandwich, or ham sandwich. He is not sure whether he wants apple juice, milk, or water to drink. If Ty is sure he wants to order one sandwich and one drink, how many different combinations can he choose from?

    (A)  6

    (B)  9

    (C)  12

    (D)  15

 HINT

Drawing a diagram will help you answer this question.

2.  Raisa is painting shapes to hang in her room. She has three shapes: a triangle, a square, and a circle. She has four colors: pink, blue, yellow, and green. How many combinations of shapes and colors does she have?

    (A)  4

    (B)  8

    (C)  10

    (D)  12

 HINT

Remember to draw a diagram and count each line.

# Practice Questions

## End-of-Chapter Practice Problems

**DIRECTIONS:**

Choose the best of the answer choices given for each of the following problems. Fill in the circle next to your choice.

The ski club uses this phone tree to remind members about upcoming ski trips.

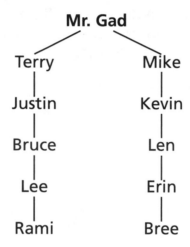

**Mr. Gad**

Terry          Mike

Justin          Kevin

Bruce          Len

Lee          Erin

Rami          Bree

Mr. Gad calls Terry and Mike, and then each student calls the person whose name is listed under his or her name. This continues until every student is called.

1. Which student will Justin call?

   Ⓐ Terry

   🅑 Bruce

   Ⓒ Len

   Ⓓ Kevin

 HINT

Remember that Justin will call the person whose name is underneath his name.

2.  **Which student will Mike call?**

    (A)  Kevin

    (B)  Len

    (C)  Terry

    (D)  Justin

HINT

Mike will call the student whose name is underneath his name.

3.  **Sasha has three T-shirts and two pairs of shorts. How many combinations of T-shirts and shorts does she have?**

    (A)  3

    (B)  4

    (C)  5

    (D)  6

HINT

Remember to make a diagram and then count the lines.

**Denise made this Venn diagram to compare her two best friends.**

**4.   What is one thing that May and Chris have in common?**

Ⓐ  They both play soccer.

●  They both live on Elm Street.

Ⓒ  They both have green eyes.

Ⓓ  They both read novels.

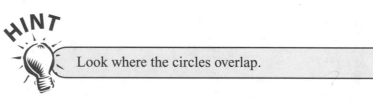

Look where the circles overlap.

**5.   What can Denise most likely conclude from her survey?**

Ⓐ  May reads more than Chris.

Ⓑ  Her friends like to play different games.

Ⓒ  Chris is older than May.

Ⓓ  Her friends both live near her.

Look at the answer choices carefully. Only one of them is true.

# New Jersey Assessment of Skills and Knowledge

**MATHEMATICS** Grade 3

## Practice Test 1

# DIRECTIONS:

**When you are taking this test, remember these important things:**

1. Read each question carefully and think about the answer.

2. If you do not know the answer to a question, go on to the next question. You may come back to the skipped question later if you have time.

3. When you see a STOP sign (STOP), do **not** turn the page until you are told to do so.

# Session 1

# Directions for Students:

This section of the test has 6 multiple-choice questions. You will fill in the circle next to the answer you choose. You may NOT use a calculator.

1.  **Find the exact number: 280 + 50**

    $$\begin{array}{r} \overset{1}{280} \\ + 50 \\ \hline 330 \end{array}$$

    Ⓐ **310**

    Ⓑ **320**

    ● **330**

    Ⓓ **340**

2. **Find the exact answer: 123 + 298 + 52**

   Ⓐ **370**

   Ⓑ **470**

   ⦿ **473**

   Ⓓ **482**

$$
\begin{array}{r}
+128 \\
+252 \\
52 \\
\hline
304
\end{array}
$$

$$
\begin{array}{r}
123 \\
+298 \\
\hline
421 \\
+52 \\
\hline
473
\end{array}
$$

3.  **Estimate 897 − 134. The difference is between which numbers?**

    Ⓐ **400 and 600**

    ● **700 and 900**

    Ⓒ **1,100 and 1,300**

    Ⓓ **1,200 and 1,400**

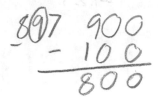

4.  **Estimate 42 × 6. The product is approximately what number?**

    Ⓐ **168**

    ● **240**

    Ⓒ **292**

    Ⓓ **300**

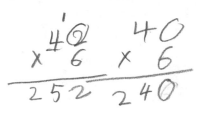

5. Sydney has a coin collection. She has 28 gold coins, 15 silver coins, and 42 bronze coins. How many coins does Sydney have in all?

Ⓐ **83**

Ⓑ **84**

● **85**

Ⓓ **86**

$$
\begin{array}{r}
1\ \ \\
4\ 2 \\
+\ 2\ 8 \\
\hline
7\ 0 \\
+\ 1\ 5 \\
\hline
8\ 5
\end{array}
$$

6.  **Which number below is an even number?**

 Ⓐ 523

 Ⓑ 127

 Ⓒ 98

 Ⓓ 71

**If you have time, you may review your work in this section only.**

**DO NOT GO ON UNTIL YOU ARE TOLD TO DO SO.**

# Session 2

## Directions for Students:

You are allowed to use a calculator for the following multiple-choice and open-ended items. You may also use the ruler and colored shapes.

7. **According to the bar graph below, how many people were at the park during April?**

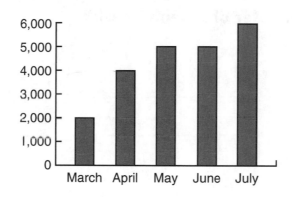

Number of People at the Park

Ⓐ **3,000**

● **4,000**

Ⓒ **5,000**

Ⓓ **6,000**

8. Joseph wants to put a border around the outside of the top of his desk. The top of the desk is shown below.

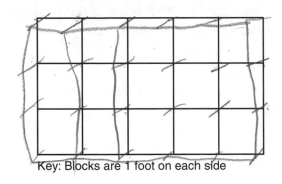

Key: Blocks are 1 foot on each side

**What is the perimeter of Joseph's desk?**

Ⓐ **6 feet**

Ⓑ **10 feet**

Ⓒ **15 feet**

Ⓓ **16 feet**

9. In the winter, some monarch butterflies travel 1,900 miles to a warmer place. What is the value of the 1 in 1,900?

Ⓐ 1 thousand

Ⓑ 1 hundred

Ⓒ 1 ten

Ⓓ 1 one

## 10. Which of these letters has a line of symmetry?

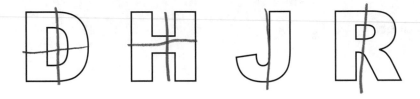

Ⓐ **D**

Ⓑ **H**

Ⓒ **J**

Ⓓ **R**

11. Use your ruler to answer this question. To the nearest inch, what is the length of the line segment AB?

Ⓐ 1 in.

● 2 in.

Ⓒ 3 in.

Ⓓ 4 in.

**12. Look at the pattern below.**

# B E H J B E H J B E H

**What is the next letter?**

Ⓐ **B**

Ⓑ **E**

Ⓒ **H**

● **J**

# Directions for the Open-Ended Question

The following question is an open-ended question. Remember to:

- Read the question carefully and think about the answer.

- Answer all the parts of the question.

- Show your work or explain your answer.

You can answer the question by using words, tables, diagrams, OR pictures. You may use your calculator, ruler, and colored shapes.

13. A machine charges 95¢ for a box of crackers and accepts only nickels, dimes, and quarters. The machine requires exact change.

What combination of coins could you put in the machine to get a box of crackers?

Show your work or explain your answer.

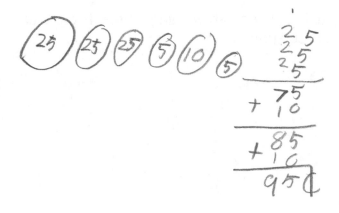

$$
\begin{array}{r}
2\,5 \\
2\,5 \\
2\,5 \\
\hline
+\ 7\,5 \\
1\,0 \\
\hline
+\ 8\,5 \\
1\,0 \\
\hline
9\,5¢
\end{array}
$$

If you have time, you may review your work in this section only.

DO NOT GO ON
UNTIL YOU ARE
TOLD TO DO SO.

# Session 3

## Directions for Students

You are allowed to use a calculator for the following multiple-choice and open-ended items. You may also use the ruler and colored shapes.

14. **There are 20 blue straws and 4 green straws in a bag. What are the chances of picking a green straw if you reach into the bag and pick one without looking?**

    Ⓐ **1 out of 4**

    Ⓑ **1 out of 20**

    Ⓒ **4 out of 24**

    Ⓓ **16 out of 24**

**15. Compare the shaded regions. Which symbol belongs in the box?**

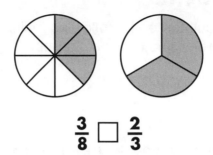

$$\frac{3}{8} \ \Box \ \frac{2}{3}$$

Ⓐ  <

Ⓑ  >

Ⓒ  =

Ⓓ  **None of the above**

16. **What is the name of the figure shown below?**

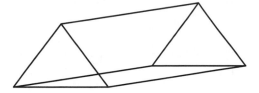

- Ⓐ **cube**

- Ⓑ **sphere**

- Ⓒ **triangular prism**

- Ⓓ **rectangular prism**

**17. What number should go in the box in 7 + ☐ = 15?**

ⓐ **6**

ⓑ **7**

◉ **8**

ⓓ **9**

**18. Which rule is assigned to the input numbers in order to get the output numbers?**

| Input | Output |
|:-----:|:------:|
| 12 | 8 |
| 11 | 7 |
| 10 | 6 |
| 9 | 5 |

Ⓐ **Add 4**

Ⓑ **Subtract 4**

Ⓒ **Multiply by 2**

Ⓓ **Divide by 2**

**19. When the Boy Scouts are planning an activity, Mr. Miller calls Brian and Mark. Each of them calls the person whose name is listed under his or her name. This continues until every student is called.**

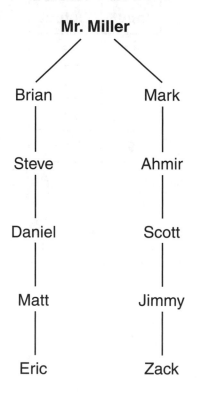

**Which boy does Brian call?**

Ⓐ **Steve**

Ⓑ **Matt**

Ⓒ **Daniel**

Ⓓ **Ahmir**

20. A machine charges 45¢ to play a game, and it takes only nickels, dimes, and quarters. Marla wants to play the game. Which combination of coins should she use?

21. Matt has 30 stickers. His brother gave him some more stickers. He now has 72 stickers. Which number sentence could you use to find how many stickers his brother gave to him?

Ⓐ $30 + 72 = \square$

Ⓑ $72 - 30 = \square$

Ⓒ $30 \times \square = 72$

Ⓓ $72 + \square = 30$

# Directions for the Open-Ended Question

The following question is an open-ended question. Remember to:

- Read the question carefully and think about the answer.

- Answer all the parts of the question.

- Show your work or explain your answer.

You can answer the question by using words, tables, diagrams, OR pictures. You may use your calculator, ruler, and colored shapes.

**22. Look at the figures below.**

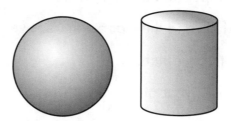

- **How many faces does each figure have?**

The sphere has zero faces.
The cilinder has tuo faces.

- **Write one way the figures are the same.**

_____

_____

- **Write one way the figures are different.**

The cilinder has faces the
spere doesn't.

**If you have time, you may review your work in this section only.**

**DO NOT GO ON
UNTIL YOU ARE
TOLD TO DO SO.**

# Session 4

## Directions for Students

You are allowed to use a calculator for the following multiple-choice and open-ended items. You may also use the ruler and colored shapes.

**23. Which picture shows a flip?**

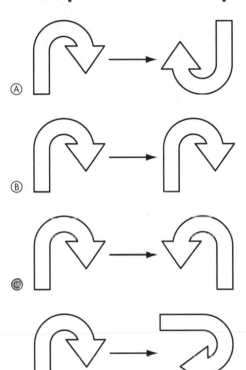

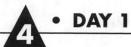 
**24. What shape has four sides that must be equal?**

Ⓐ **rectangle**

Ⓑ **octagon**

Ⓒ **pentagon**

Ⓓ **square**

**25. According to the following bar graph, how many miles did Rex run on Day 3?**

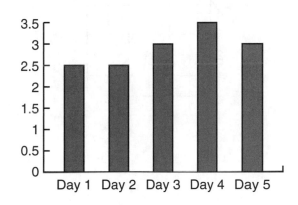

Rex's Running Distances in Miles

Ⓐ **2**

Ⓑ **2.5**

Ⓒ **3**

Ⓓ **3.5**

26. Which ordered pair shows the location of Shelly's school?

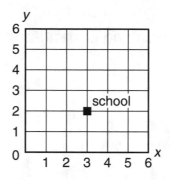

Ⓐ (2, 3)

Ⓑ (3, 2)

Ⓒ (3, 3)

Ⓓ (2, 2)

**27. When 14 is dropped into the following machine, it comes out as 7.**

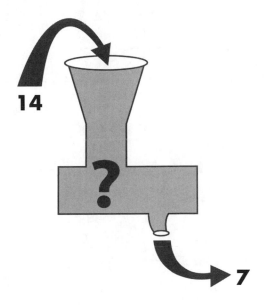

**When 16 is dropped in, it comes out as 8.**

**When 4 is dropped in, it comes out as 2.**

**If 8 is dropped into the machine, what number will it come out as?**

Ⓐ **2**

Ⓑ **4**

Ⓒ **5**

Ⓓ **6**

**28. What does the *n* equal in 4 + *n* = 15?**

    Ⓐ **9**

    Ⓑ **10**

    Ⓒ **11**

    Ⓓ **12**

## 29. How much would it cost to buy 3 tickets to the play?

| Number of Tickets to a Play | Cost |
|---|---|
| 1 | $7.50 |
| 2 | $14.00 |
| 3 | $20.00 |
| 4 | $25.00 |

Ⓐ **$7.50**

Ⓑ **$14.00**

◉ **$20.00**

Ⓓ **$25.00**

**30.** The pictograph below shows how many students are in Martina's grade.

Key: ▐ = 10 students

**How many students are in Martina's grade?**

Ⓐ **10**

Ⓑ **100**

Ⓒ **1,000**

Ⓓ **10,000**

# Directions for the Open-Ended Question

The following question is an open-ended question. Remember to:

- Read the question carefully and think about the answer.

- Answer all the parts of the question.

- Show your work or explain your answer.

You can answer the question by using words, tables, diagrams, OR pictures. You may use your calculator, ruler, and colored shapes.

**31.** Your class is trying to raise money to go on a class trip. The record of the total amount of money your class has at the end of each week is shown in the chart below.

| Week | 1 | 2 | 3 | 4 | 5 |
|---|---|---|---|---|---|
| Total amount of money saved | $10.50 | $14.75 | $19.00 | $23.25 | |

If you continue saving money following this pattern, how much money will you have at the end of Week 5? Explain the pattern you used to get your answer.

$$14.75$$
$$-10.50$$
$$04.25$$

$$13.25$$
$$-9.00$$
$$14.25$$
$$-4.25$$
$$10.00$$

**CLOSE YOUR BOOK.**

# New Jersey Assessment of Skills and Knowledge

**MATHEMATICS** Grade 3

Practice Test 2

# DIRECTIONS

**When you are taking this test, remember these important things:**

1. Read each question carefully and think about the answer.

2. If you do not know the answer to a question, go on to the next question. You may come back to the skipped question later if you have time.

3. When you see a STOP sign **STOP**, do **not** turn the page until you are told to do so.

## Session 1

## Directions for Students:

This section of the test has 6 multiple-choice questions. You will fill in the circle next to the answer you choose. You may NOT use a calculator.

1. **Find the exact number: 700 − 125**

   Ⓐ **475**

   Ⓑ **500**

   ● **575**

   Ⓓ **625**

2.  **Estimate 245 + 672. The sum is between which numbers?**

Ⓐ  **600 and 800**

●  **800 and 1,000**

©  **1,000 and 1,200**

Ⓓ  **1,300 and 1,500**

3.  **Find the exact number: 72 ÷ 9**

    Ⓐ **6**

    Ⓑ **7**

    Ⓒ **8**

    Ⓓ **9**

4. **Which number below is an odd number?**

Ⓐ **58**

Ⓑ **76**

Ⓒ **122**

● **201**

**5.** **Find the exact difference: 487 − 38**

   Ⓐ **348**

   Ⓑ **449**

   Ⓒ **450**

   Ⓓ **525**

6. **Estimate 410 − 292. The difference is between which numbers?**

   Ⓐ **100 and 200**

   Ⓑ **200 and 300**

   Ⓒ **300 and 400**

   Ⓓ **400 and 500**

If you have time, you may review your work in this section only.

**DO NOT GO ON UNTIL YOU ARE TOLD TO DO SO.**

# Session 2

## Directions for Students

You are allowed to use a calculator for the following multiple-choice and open-ended items. You may also use the ruler and colored shapes.

7. **Margaret's family moved to another state 628 miles away. What is the value of 2 in the number 628?**

   Ⓐ **2 thousands**

   Ⓑ **2 hundreds**

   ● **2 tens**

   Ⓓ **2 ones**

8. **Compare the shaded regions. Which symbol belongs in the box?**

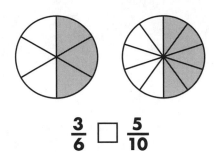

$$\frac{3}{6} \ \square \ \frac{5}{10}$$

Ⓐ  <

Ⓑ  >

Ⓒ  =

Ⓓ  **None of the above**

**9.** **Which of these shapes has a line of symmetry?**

Ⓐ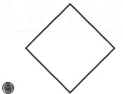

Ⓑ

Ⓒ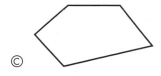

Ⓓ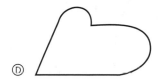

10. Greg needs to pay a toll of 80¢ to drive on a new road. The toll machine accepts only nickels, dimes, and quarters. The machine requires exact change. What combination of coins should Greg use?

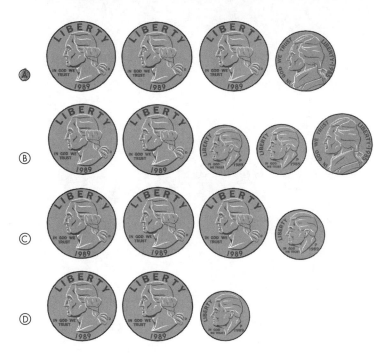

## 11. Which of these is a line?

Ⓐ •————————•

Ⓑ ◄————————•

Ⓒ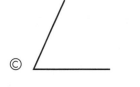

Ⓓ ◄————————►

12. Which unit of measure would you use to measure to distance from your house to your friend's house across town?

Ⓐ inches

Ⓑ feet

Ⓒ yards

Ⓓ miles

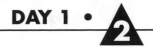

# Directions for the Open-Ended Question

The following question is an open-ended question. Remember to:

- Read the question carefully and think about the answer.

- Answer all the parts of the question.

- Show your work or explain your answer.

You can answer the question by using words, tables, diagrams, OR pictures. You may use your calculator, ruler, and colored shapes.

13. The table below shows how many gallons of milk a store sold each day during one week.

| Day | Gallons of Milk Sold |
|---|---|
| Monday | 5 |
| Tuesday | 8 |
| Wednesday | 11 |
| Thursday | 14 |
| Friday | |

If the pattern continued, how many gallons of milk did the store sell on Friday?

Show your work or explain your answer.

$$\begin{array}{r} 5 \\ +3 \\ \hline 8 \end{array} \qquad \begin{array}{r} 11 \\ +3 \\ \hline 14 \end{array} \qquad 17$$

If you have time, you may review your work in this section only.

**DO NOT GO ON UNTIL YOU ARE TOLD TO DO SO.**

# Session 3

# Directions for Students

You are allowed to use a calculator for the following multiple-choice and open-ended items. You may also use the ruler and colored shapes.

**14. Which pair of shapes is the same size and shape?**

Ⓐ

Ⓑ

Ⓒ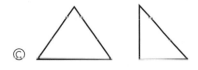

Ⓓ

**15. According to the following bar graph, what was Eric's grade on Test 5?**

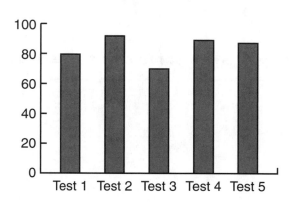

Eric's Test Grades

Ⓐ **70**

Ⓑ **75**

◉ **80**

Ⓓ **85**

**16. How many books did Ken read, according to the following pictograph?**

Key: 📖 = 2 books

(A) **3**

● **6**

(C) **8**

(D) **9**

**17. Which ordered pair shows the location of Point *B*?**

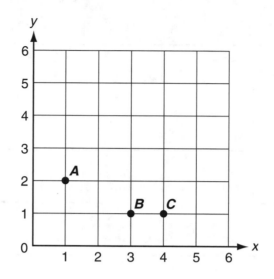

Ⓐ **(3, 1)**

Ⓑ **(1, 3)**

Ⓒ **(2, 1)**

Ⓓ **(1, 2)**

**18. Use your ruler to answer this question. To the nearest centimeter, what is the length of line segment *CD*?**

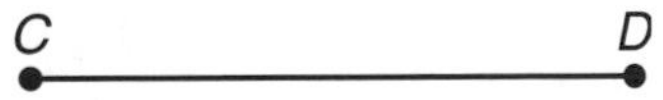

C ●─────────────● D

Ⓐ **16 cm**

Ⓑ **8 cm**

⬤ **4 cm**

Ⓓ **2 cm**

19. Chris can wear tan pants or black pants to school. He can also wear a blue or black jacket. How many combinations of outfits does Chris have?

Ⓐ **2**

Ⓑ **4**

Ⓒ **6**

Ⓓ **8**

**20. What does the *p* equal in $16 - p = 9$**

Ⓐ **3**

Ⓑ **5**

◉ **7**

Ⓓ **8**

21. Sidney has a toy car collection. He has 32 red cars, 24 blue cars, and 12 green cars. How many cars does he have in all?

Ⓐ 64

Ⓑ 66

◉ 68

Ⓓ 70

# Directions for the Open-Ended Question

The following question is an open-ended question. Remember to:

- Read the question carefully and think about the answer.

- Answer all the parts of the question.

- Show your work or explain your answer.

You can answer the question by using words, tables, diagrams, OR pictures. You may use your calculator, ruler, and colored shapes.

**22. Look at the figures below. Name each figure.**

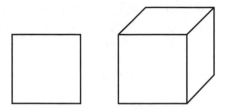

- **How many corners does each figure have?**
- **Write one way that the figures are the same.**
- **Write one way that the figures are different.**

The squre has four corners. The cub has 8 corners. They both have an eqle amount of corners

**If you have time, you may review your work in this section only.**

**Page 230**

DO NOT GO ON
UNTIL YOU ARE
TOLD TO DO SO.

# Session 4

# Directions for Students

You are allowed to use a calculator for the following multiple-choice and open-ended items. You may also use the ruler and colored shapes.

**23. Clarissa made this Venn diagram to compare her mother and her father.**

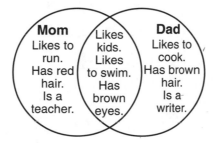

**What can Clarissa conclude from her Venn diagram?**

Ⓐ **Both Mom and Dad are teachers.**

Ⓑ **Both Mom and Dad like to cook.**

Ⓒ **Both Mom and Dad have brown eyes.**

Ⓓ **Both Mom and Dad have red hair.**

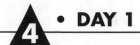 

**24.** Which rule is assigned to the *x* column to get the number in the *y* column?

| x | y |
|---|---|
| 4 | 1 |
| 5 | 2 |
| 6 | 3 |
| 7 | 4 |
| 8 | 5 |

Ⓐ **Add 1**

Ⓑ **Subtract 3**

Ⓒ **Multiply by 3**

Ⓓ **Divide by 2**

**25. When 30 is dropped into this machine, it comes out 20.**

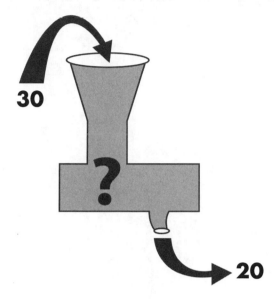

**When 40 is dropped in, it comes out 30.**

**When 15 is dropped in, it comes out 5.**

**If 20 is dropped into the machine, what number will come out?**

Ⓐ **0**

Ⓑ **5**

Ⓒ **10**

Ⓓ **15**

26. Carmen has 10 red beads, 5 blue beads, and 5 pink beads in a bag. What are the chances of picking a pink bead if she reaches into the bag and picks one without looking?

Ⓐ 1 out of 5

Ⓑ 5 out of 10

⬤ 5 out of 20

Ⓓ 10 out of 20

27. If $13 + \Box = 20$, what is the value of $\Box$?

Ⓐ 4

Ⓑ 5

Ⓒ 6

Ⓓ 7

**28. Which rule is assigned to the input numbers in order to get the output numbers?**

| Input | Output |
|:-----:|:------:|
| 4 | 8 |
| 5 | 10 |
| 6 | 12 |
| 7 | 14 |

Ⓐ **Add 4**

Ⓑ **Subtract 5**

Ⓒ **Multiply by 2**

Ⓓ **Divide by 2**

**29.** If $265 \times \square = 0$, then what is the value of $\square$?

Ⓐ  −1

Ⓑ  **0**

Ⓒ  **1**

Ⓓ  **265**

30. The table below shows the number of students in Brenda's class for several years.

| Year | Number of Students |
|---|---|
| 1 | 24 |
| 2 | 16 |
| 3 | 20 |
| 4 | 25 |

**How many students were in Brenda's class in year 2?**

Ⓐ **16**

Ⓑ **20**

Ⓒ **24**

Ⓓ **25**

# Directions for the Open-Ended Question

The following question is an open-ended question. Remember to:

- Read the question carefully and think about the answer.

- Answer all the parts of the question.

- Show your work or explain your answer.

You can answer the question by using words, tables, diagrams, OR pictures. You may use your calculator, ruler, and colored shapes.

**31. The bar graph below shows the number of cars sold from January until July.**

Cars Sold, January Through July

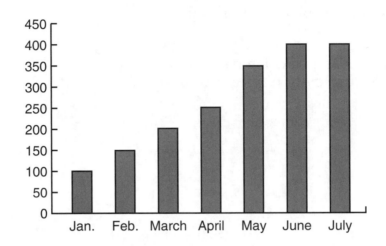

- **How many cars were sold in January?**

- **How many cars were sold in July?**

- **How do car sales change as the weather gets warmer?**

100 cars were sold in Jan.
400 cars were sold in July.
The sales get higer.

CLOSE YOUR
BOOK.

# Answer Key
# Chapter 1 Answer Explanations

## Practice 1: Even and Odd Numbers

**1. B**

Remember that even numbers end in 0, 2, 4, 6, or 8. Answer choice B, 278, is an even number.

**2. D**

Odd numbers end in 1, 3, 5, 7, or 9. Answer choice D, 313, is an odd number.

## Practice 2: Whole Numbers and Place Value

**1. B**

Nine is in the hundreds place. Answer choice B is correct.

**2. A**

The 1 in the number 1,803 is in the thousands place. The 8 is in the hundreds place, the 0 is in the tens place, and the 3 is in the ones place.

## Practice 3: Fractions

**1. D**

A whole number doesn't have a fraction. Answer choice D, 312, is the only whole number.

**2. C**

A fraction has a numerator and a denominator. Answer choice C is a fraction.

## Practice 4:  Comparing Fraction Sizes

**1.   B**

You can tell from the shaded areas that $\frac{2}{3}$ is greater than $\frac{1}{2}$. Answer choice B is correct.

**2.   A**

Since the denominators are the same, it's easy to tell that $\frac{8}{12}$ is less than $\frac{10}{12}$, since 8 is less than 10. This is also seen from the shaded regions in the figure.

## Practice 5:  Decimals

**1.   D**

Remember that place values after a decimal end in "th." In the number .98, the 8 is in the hundredths place.

**2.   C**

The 3 in the number .34 is in the tenths place.

## End-of-Chapter Practice Problems

**1.   A**

You can see from the shaded regions that $\frac{1}{4}$ is less than $\frac{1}{2}$.

**2.   A**

The number 2 in 128,543 is in the ten thousands place, so its value is 2 ten thousands, or 20 thousands. Be careful here! Twenty thousand*ths* would refer to a decimal.

**3.   C**

Odd numbers end in 1, 3, 5, 7, or 9. The number 45, answer choice C, is an odd number.

**4. B**

Fractions have a numerator and a denominator.

**5. A**

You can tell from the shaded regions that $\frac{1}{4}$ is less than $\frac{1}{3}$.

**6. D**

In the decimal .25, 5 is in the hundredths place.

**7. B**

A decimal has a point. Answer choice B, .19, is the only answer option that is a decimal. Answer choice A, 1.45, is a mixed decimal—it has a whole number part (1) and a decimal part (.45).

**8. B**

These fractions have the same denominator, so just compare the numerators. The fraction with the larger numerator is greater.

**9. B**

The 7 in the number 2,710 is in the hundreds place.

**10. A**

The number 212, answer choice A, is the only answer choice that ends in 0, 2, 4, 6, or 8.

# Chapter 2 Answer Explanations

## Practice 6: Adding and Subtracting Numbers

**1. C**

If you add 80 and 20, you get 100. Answer choice C is correct.

**2. B**

If you subtract 30 from 100, you get 70. Answer choice B is correct.

**3. B**

If you had trouble adding three numbers, you could always add two numbers together and then add the third. For instance, 82 + 79 = 161, and 161 + 90 = 251.

**4. C**

If you add 190 + 45 + 62, you get 297. Answer choice C is correct.

**5. B**

Julie had 35 pencils. She gave 25 away (10 to her sister and 15 to her friend). When you subject 25 from 35, you get 10. Julie has 10 pencils left.

## Practice 7:  Multiplying and Dividing Numbers

**1. D**

You should be able to do this problem by using mental math. Dividing 90 by 9 gives you 10.

**2. D**

When you multiply 14 by 8, you get 112. Answer choice D is correct.

**3. B**

To find out how many flowers Tara needs, you need to multiply 18 by 3. The answer is 54. Tara needs 54 flowers.

## Practice 8:  Counting Money

**1. C**

The value of two quarters is 50 cents. If you add a dime and a nickel to this value, you will get 65 cents.

2.  Open-ended

    **Sample answer:** I would need 1 quarter and 1 dime to play the pinball
    machine. Also acceptable is 1 quarter and 2 nickels or 3
    dimes and 1 nickel, among other solutions.

## End-of-Chapter Practice Problems

1.  **C**

    When you add 210 and 80, you get 290. Answer choice C is correct.

2.  **D**

    When you divide 8 into 128, you get 16. Answer choice D is correct.

3.  **D**

    If you add 34, 28, and 25 correctly, your answer should be 87.

4.  **A**

    The number 18 goes into 108 six times. Answer choice A is correct.

5.  Open-ended

    **Sample answer:** I could use 3 quarters to get into the fair.
    Alternative answers are 2 quarters, 2 dimes, and
    1 nickel, or 7 dimes and 1 nickel, among other solutions.

6.  **D**

    The number 72 multiplied by 6 is 432. You might also be able to do this
    by adding 72 + 72 + 72 + 72 + 72 + 72.

7.  **C**

    If you can add 12 and 22 by using mental math, this problem will be
    easier. If you add 12 and 22, you get 34. Then subtract 34 from 40. The
    answer is 6.

**8.  C**

You might also be able to do this problem by using mental math. You probably know that 90 subtracted from 100 is 10, so 89 subtracted from 100 is 11.

**9.  C**

You can reach this answer by adding the three numbers together at once, or by adding 22 and 56 and then adding this sum (78) to 90.

**10.  C**

If you subtract 75 from 500, you get 425. Answer choice C is correct.

# Chapter 3 Answer Explanations

**Practice 9:  Estimating Addition**

**1.   C**

The number 256 rounded to the nearest hundred is 300. The number 64 rounded to the nearest 10 is 60. If you add 300 + 60, you get 360. This number is between the numbers in answer choice C, 301 and 400.

**2.   C**

The number 120 rounded to the nearest hundred is 100. The number 471 rounded to the nearest hundred is 500. If you add 100 + 500, you get 600. This number is between 500 and 699, the range in answer choice C.

**Practice 10:  Estimating Subtraction**

**1.   B**

When you round 520 to the nearest hundred, you get 500. When you round 92 to the nearest ten, you get 90. When you subtract these numbers, the answer is 410. Answer choice B is correct.

2. **D**

When you round 980 to the nearest hundred, you get 1,000. When you round 670 to the nearest hundred, you get 700. If you subtract 1,000 from 700, you get 300. Answer choice D is correct.

## Practice 11: Estimating Multiplication

1. **C**

If you round 102 to 100 and multiply 100 by 2, you get 200. Answer choice C is correct.

2. **C**

If you round 56 to 60 and multiply 60 by 3, you get 180. Answer choice C is correct.

## Practice 12: Estimating Division

1. **B**

If you round 43 to 40 and divide 40 by 4, you get 10. Answer choice B is correct.

2. **B**

If you round 38 to 40 and divide by 2, you get 20. Answer choice B is correct.

## End-of-Chapter Practice Problems

1. **A**

If you round 340 to 300 and round 190 to 200 and subtract 200 from 300, you get 100.

2. **A**

If you round 124 to 100 and round 65 to 70 and add them, the sum is 170.

3.  **C**

    The number 4 goes into 80 twenty times.

4.  **C**

    If you round 856 to the nearest hundred, you get 900. If you round 91 to the nearest 10, you get 90. If you subtract 90 from 900, you get 810.

5.  **A**

    The number 256 rounded to the nearest hundred is 300. The number 110 rounded to the nearest hundred is 100. If you add 300 and 100, you get 400.

6.  **A**

    If you round 24 to 20 and multiply by 3, you get 60.

# Chapter 4 Answer Explanations

**Practice 13: Lines**

1.  **A**

    A line segment is part of a line. It has two endpoints. Answer choice A is a line segment.

2.  **C**

    The points at the end of a line segment are called endpoints. Answer choice C is correct.

**Practice 14: Two-Dimensional Shapes**

1.  **B**

    A hexagon has six sides that do not have to be the same length. Answer choice B is a hexagon.

2. **B**

An octagon has eight sides that do not have to be equal. Answer choice B is the correct answer.

## Practice 15: Three-Dimensional Shapes

1. **A**

A cube looks like a block. Answer choice A is a cube.

2. **D**

A sphere looks like a ball and doesn't have a face.

## Practice 16: Lines of Symmetry

1. **B**

A rectangle has two lines of symmetry. You can draw a dotted line down the middle on the top or on the side and the two halves are exactly the same.

2. **C**

The letter W has a line of symmetry. Both halves are exactly the same.

## Practice 17: Congruent Shapes

1. **B**

The triangles in answer choice B are exactly the same (but flipped). They are congruent.

2. **C**

Answer choice C shows a pair of shapes that are not the same.

### End-of-Chapter Practice Problems

1.  **A**

    The triangle in answer choice A is facing in a different direction than the triangle in the question, but it is congruent.

2.  **A**

    The letter A is the only letter shown that has a line of symmetry. It can be divided in half and the halves are exactly the same.

3.  **B**

    A triangular prism looks like a pyramid. Answer choice B shows a pyramid.

4.  **C**

    An angle is shown in this question.

5.  **D**

    A triangle has three sides that do not have to be equal. Answer choice D is correct.

6.  **D**

    A rectangular prism looks like a box. It also looks like a three-dimensional rectangle.

7.  **C**

    A pentagon has five sides. Only C shows a five-sided figure.

8.  Open-ended    rectangular prism; cube

    **Sample answer:** Each figure has six faces. This makes them alike. They are also alike in that they each have corners. They are different in that a rectangular prism, like a rectangle, has two pairs of sides the same length. For a cube, all sides are the same size, and so are the faces and edges.

# Chapter 5 Answer Explanations

## Practice 18: Moving Shapes

**1. B**

Answer choice B is the only one that does not show a turn. And remember that a slide does not turn.

**2. D**

A flip is a reflection. When a shape is flipped, it should look upside-down, or like a mirror image.

**3. C**

Answer choice A is a vertical flip (it is a reflection). Answer choices B and D are slides. Answer choice C shows a turn.

## Practice 19: Coordinate Grids

**1. C**

Katie's school is located at coordinate 3 on the *x*-axis and coordinate 1 on the *y*-axis, or at (3, 1).

**2. B**

Katie's house is located at coordinate 2 on the *x*-axis and coordinate 3 on the *y*-axis.

**3. D**

Point *A* is 1 place over on the *x*-axis and 1 place up on the *y*-axis.

## End-of-Chapter Practice Problems

**1. D**

Answer choice D is the only answer choice in which the shape is not turned.

**2. C**

To get to Marty's house, you have to move 2 places on the *x*-axis and 5 places on the *y*-axis.

**3. D**

To get to the store, you have to move 5 places on the *x*-axis and 2 places on the *y*-axis.

**4. Open-ended**

**Sample answer:** Point *A* is located at (1, 4). You have to move 1 place over on the *x*-axis and 4 places up on the *y*-axis.

**5.**

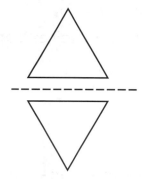

# Chapter 6 Answer Explanations

**Practice 20: Units of Measurement**

**1. B**

It might seem like a pretty long way from your bedroom floor to the ceiling, but try to remember the size of each unit of measurement. Centimeters are too tiny to use. Miles and kilometers are used for very long distances, so they are too big. The best answer choice is feet.

2.   **A**

Think of how big a penny is. It's pretty small. Right away, you should be able to see that meters, yards, and miles are far too big to measure such a small object. Centimeters is the correct choice.

## Practice 21:  Weight

1.   **D**

Because a house is so large, you would want to use the largest unit of measurement listed in the answer choices. The largest one is tons, and it is the best answer.

2.   **B**

Five grams is a very small number, meaning that the object being measured is very small. The smallest object listed in the answer choices is a nickel.

## Practice 22:  Capacity

1.   **B**

The end of the shaded area falls right between 4 pints and 6 pints. This means that the liquid in the measure is about 5 pints.

2.   **D**

A swimming pool holds a lot of water. If you measured the amount of water in a pool in cups, it would be a very high number. Pints and quarts are also a little too small to use. The best answer is gallons.

## Practice 23:  Perimeter and Area

1.   **D**

To find the perimeter of the triangle, you should add together all of the sides in the same way you added together all of the blocks around the pool. When you add 12 + 13, you get 25. Then you need to add this sum to the measurement of the last side. 25 + 5 = 30. The perimeter of the triangle is 30 inches.

2.  **B**

Remember that area is the amount of space an object covers. This question asks you to figure out the area of the shaded blocks. If you count all of the shaded blocks, you can see that they cover an area of 14 blocks.

3.  **D**

For this shaded triangle, you have to add half blocks together to make whole ones. There are 4 half blocks shaded. When you add two halves together, you get one whole block. When you add 4 half blocks together, you get 2. Add these 2 blocks to the other shaded blocks. You can see that the triangle covers an area of 8 shaded blocks altogether.

## End-of-Chapter Practice Problems

1.  **C**

The line measures $3\frac{1}{2}$ inches. To get the best answer, make sure that you line up your ruler correctly when you are measuring.

2.  **A**

Remember what you learned about metric units? Some are used to measure length, and some are used to measure weight. Centimeters and meters are used for length, so we know that Lisa would not use them to see how much her dog weighs. Grams measure very small objects. Because you already know that Lisa's dog weighs 32 pounds, you would probably not want to use grams to weigh her dog. One kilogram is the same as about 2 pounds and would be the perfect metric unit to measure the weight of Lisa's dog.

3.  **C**

By looking at the shaded area, you can see that it falls between the 1 and the 2. This means that there are $1\frac{1}{2}$ cups of water in Rich's pitcher.

4.  **C**

    Each long side of the object has 5 unit edges. $5 + 5 = 10$. The other two sides have 4 unit edges each. $4 + 4 = 8$. Now we need to add the sums together. $10 + 8 = 18$. The object has a perimeter of 18 units.

5.  **D**

    Each side of this triangle measures $1\frac{1}{2}$ inches. This means that when you add them all together, you will see that the perimeter of the triangle is $4\frac{1}{2}$ inches.

6.  **A**

    Feet and inches are not used to measure long distances. Even yards would not be large enough. The best way to measure the distance from one town to another is in miles.

7.  **D**

    By counting all of the shaded blocks, you can see that the object covers a space of 24 blocks.

8.  **B**

    The first figure has an area of 20 blocks. The figure in choice A has 16 blocks. This is not the answer. The figure in choice C also has 16 blocks. The figure in choice D has 24 blocks. Choice B has exactly 20 blocks, so it covers the same area as the figure in the question.

# Chapter 7 Answer Explanations

**Practice 24: Patterns**

1.  Open-ended

    **Sample answer:** Each week, 50¢ is saved. In Week 4, $3.00 is saved, so in Week 5, $3.50 will have been saved.

2.  **B**

The pattern is A C E G; after the letter A comes the letter C.

### Practice 25:  Function Machine

1.  **B**

The numbers decrease by 3, so if 8 is dropped into the machine, it will come out as 5.

2.  **D**

The numbers are increased by 4, so if 18 is dropped into the machine, it will come out as 22.

### Practice 26:  Input/Output Tables and T-Charts

1.  **C**

The numbers are each multiplied by 2. For example, $7 \times 2 = 14$.

2.  **B**

The numbers in the $y$ column of the T-chart are two less than those in the $x$ column. For example, $4 - 2 = 2$.

### Practice 27:  Open Sentences

1.  **C**

If you add 16 to 5, you get 21.

2.  **C**

If you subtract 9 from 32, you get 23.

3.  **B**

If you add 11 to 13, you get 24.

**4. C**

If you subtract 14 from 98, you get 84.

## Practice 28: Number Sentences

**1. B**

If you take 24 (the number he already had) and add it to the number of crayons Peter's mother gave him, you get 36 (the number he has now).

**2. C**

If you subtract 24 (the number of marbles Tara gave away) from 68 (the number she started with), you get how many she has now.

## Practice 29: Multiplication Rules

**1. A**

Any number multiplied by 0 is 0.

**2. C**

This question asks about the associative property. If you multiply three numbers, you can move the parentheses and still get the same answer.

**3. B**

Any number multiplied by 1 is that number.

## End-of-Chapter Practice Problems

**1. B**

The input numbers show that, in each case, 4 has been subtracted to get the numbers in the output column. For example, $14 - 4 = 10$.

**2. C**

The pattern shows that 75¢ is added each week.

**3. C**

The number 5 subtracted from 17 is 12.

**4. C**

If you add 25 to 7, you get 32.

**5. C**

To get the numbers in the second column, you have to add 8 to the numbers in the first column.

**6. C**

The function machine is subtracting 6 from the numbers put into it.

**7. B**

If you subtract 32 from 48, you get 16.

**8. Open-ended**

**Sample answer:** The value of the missing number is 0. You know this because any number multiplied by zero is zero.

**9. B**

If you add the number of tokens Renee's father gave her to 12 (the number she already had), you get 26 (the number Renee has now).

# Chapter 8 Answer Explanations

**Practice 30: Bar Graphs**

**1. C**

Look for Tuesday on the bottom of the bar graph. The bar above Tuesday goes up to 2. Ruby studied for 2 hours on Tuesday.

2. **D**

The highest bar is for Thursday. On Thursday, Ruby studied for 2.5 hours, or $2\frac{1}{2}$ hours.

## Practice 31: Probability

1. **B**

There are 10 marbles altogether, and 3 of these marbles are red. So the probability that Tina will pick a red marble is 3 out of 10.

2. **C**

There are 10 cards in a deck and 5 of the cards have diamonds on them, so the probability that the first student will pick a card with a diamond is 5 out of 10.

## End-of-Chapter Practice Problems

1. **D**

Melanie has 6 stars on the chart, and each star stands for 3 chores. If you multiply $6 \times 3$, the answer is 18.

2. **C**

There are 9 pairs of socks in Melanie's drawer and 2 of them are blue, so the probability that she will pull out a blue pair is 2 out of 9.

3. **C**

The spinner has 6 equal sections, and 2 of them are blue, so the answer is 2 out of 6.

4. **B**

The girl who runs the fastest will have the fewest minutes. Sam ran a mile in only 6 minutes, so she is the fastest runner.

# Chapter 9 Answer Explanations

**Practice 32:  Venn Diagrams and Tree Diagrams**

**1.   D**

The only answer choice that is in the overlapping area of the two circles is D: Both Casey and Ray are tall.

**2.   C**

The name under Billy's name is Kate. This is the person Billy calls.

**Practice 33:  Combinations**

**1.   B**

If you set up a diagram and draw a line from each sandwich to each drink, you should have nine lines. This is the number of combinations Ty has to choose from.

**2.   D**

In this problem, there are 12 lines in the diagram, so answer choice D is correct.

**End-of-Chapter Practice Problems**

**1.   B**

The name under Justin's name is Bruce. This is the person Justin will call.

**2.   A**

The name under Mike's name is Kevin. This is the person Mike will call.

**3.   D**

If you set up a diagram, you'll see that there are six lines. This is the number of combinations Sasha has.

**4. B**

The only answer choice in the center of the diagram is B. Both of Denise's friends live on Elm Street.

**5. B**

Denise can conclude that her friends both like to play different games.

# Practice Test 1 Answer Explanations

**1. C** (Standard Assessed: Numerical Operations)

If you add 280 and 50, the answer is 330. Answer choice C is correct.

**2. C** (Standard Assessed: Numerical Operations)

If you line up the numbers and add them correctly, the answer is 473.

**3. B** (Standard Assessed: Estimation)

Round 897 to 900. Round 134 to 100. Then subtract 100 from 900 to get 800. Answer choice B shows the correct range.

**4. B** (Standard Assessed: Estimation)

Round 42 to 40 and multiply by 6. An easy way to do this is to multiply $4 \times 6$ and add a zero.

**5. C** (Standard Assessed: Numerical Operations)

If you correctly add 28, 15, and 42, the answer is 85.

**6. C** (Standard Assessed: Number Sense)

Even numbers end in 0, 2, 4, 6, or 8.

**7. B** (Standard Assessed: Data Analysis)

The bar for April reaches up to the number 4,000 on the left.

**8. D**  (Standard Assessed: Measuring)

If you add up the number of unit edges across the bottom and top and along both sides, the answer is 16.

**9. A**  (Standard Assessed: Number Sense)

In the number 1,900, the 1 is in the thousands place, the 9 is in the hundreds place, one zero is in the tens place, and the other is in the ones place.

**10. B**  (Standard Assessed: Geometric Properties)

The only letter shown that has a line of symmetry is H. If you draw a dotted line down the center, both halves will be exactly the same.

**11. B**  (Standard Assessed: Units of Measurement)

If you use the inches part of your ruler, you'll see that the line segment is 2 inches long.

**12. D**  (Standard Assessed: Patterns)

The pattern is B E H J. After the H comes the letter J.

**13. Open-ended**   (Standard Assessed: Numerical Operations)

**Sample answer:** I used 3 quarters and 2 dimes. It is also okay to draw the coins.

**14. C**  (Standard Assessed: Probability)

If there are 24 straws in total and 4 are green, the chances of picking out a green straw are 4 out of 24.

**15. A**  (Standard Assessed: Number Sense)

If you look carefully at the shaded areas, you'll see that $\frac{3}{8}$ is less than $\frac{2}{3}$.

**16. C**  (Standard Assessed: Geometric Properties)

The three-dimensional object shown is a triangular prism.

**17. C** (Standard Assessed: Modeling)

What number added to 7 equals 15? Mental math gives you 8. This is the number that should go in the box.

**18. B** (Standard Assessed: Functions and Relationships)

Each number in the output column is four less than in the input column.

**19. A** (Standard Assessed: Discrete Mathematics)

Brian calls Steve. This is the name under Brian's name in the phone tree.

**20. B** (Standard Assessed: Numerical Operations)

The value of a quarter is 25¢. If you add two dimes to this, you have 45¢. Answer choice B is correct. The coins in answer choice A add up to 55¢. The coins in answer choice C add up to 60¢. The coins in answer choice D add up to 35¢.

**21. B** (Standard Assessed: Modeling)

We know that Matt had 30 stickers and now he has 72 stickers. The number of stickers his brother gave to him is the difference between what Matt has now and what he had before. $72 - 30 = \square$. Answer choice B is correct.

**22.** Open-ended (Standard Assessed: Geometric Properties)

**Sample answer:** The figure on the left is a sphere, and the figure on the right is a cylinder. A sphere doesn't have any faces, and the cylinder has two. The figures are the same in that they are round in appearance. They are different in that the sphere is not flat on the top and the bottom like the cylinder.

**23. C** (Standard Assessed: Transforming Shapes)

Remember that a flip is like a reflection. Answer choice C is correct.

**24. D** (Standard Assessed: Geometric Properties)

A square has four sides that are equal. A pentagon and an octagon have more sides, and they don't have to be equal. A rectangle has two pairs of equal sides, but all four don't have to be equal.

**25. C**   (Standard Assessed: Data Analysis)

If you look at the bar for Day 3, you'll see that it reaches up to the number 3. Rex ran 3 miles on Day 3.

**26. B**   (Standard Assessed: Coordinate Geometry)

If you go over 3 places on the *x*-axis and up 2 on the *y*-axis, you get to Shelly's school, at (3, 2).

**27. B**   (Standard Assessed: Functional Relationships)

All of the inputs are divided in half. If you drop 8 into the machine, it will come out as 4.

**28. C**   (Standard Assessed: Modeling)

To find the answer to this question, subtract 4 from 15.

**29. C**   (Standard Assessed: Data Analysis)

Find the number 3 on the table, and then move across to see how much they cost.

**30. B**   (Standard Assessed: Data Analysis)

If one picture of a student equals 10 students and there are 10 pictures of students in the box, there are 100 students in Martina's grade.

**31.** Open-ended   (Standard Assessed: Patterns)

**Sample answer:** The pattern is to add $4.25 each week.

$$
\begin{array}{r}
23.25 \\
+\ 4.25 \\
\hline
27.50 \\
\end{array}
$$

# Practice Test 2 Answer Explanations

1. **C** (Standard Assessed: Numerical Operations)

   If you subtract 125 from 700, you get 575. Set up the problem this way:

   ```
     700
   − 125
     575
   ```

   Remember to borrow from the 7 and then borrow from the 10 in the second column.

2. **B** (Standard Assessed: Estimation)

   Round 245 to 200 and then round 672 to 700. Answer choice B gives the correct range of numbers.

3. **C** (Standard Assessed: Numerical Operations)

   If you divide 9 into 72, the answer is 8. Use mental math.

4. **D** (Standard Assessed: Number Sense)

   Odd numbers end in 1, 3, 5, 7, or 9.

5. **B** (Standard Assessed: Numerical Operations)

   Set up the numbers so you can subtract vertically (up and down). The correct answer is B, 449.

6. **A** (Standard Assessed: Estimation)

   Round 410 to 400 and then 292 to 300. When you subtract these numbers, you get 100. Answer choice A is correct.

7. **C** (Standard Assessed: Number Sense)

   In the number 628, the 6 is in the hundreds place, the 2 is in the tens place, and the 8 is in the ones place.

8.  **C**   (Standard Assessed: Number Sense)

    If you look closely at the shaded areas, you'll see that the two fractions are equal. Also, $\frac{3}{6}$ and $\frac{5}{10}$ are both equal to $\frac{1}{2}$.

9.  **A**   (Standard Assessed: Geometric Properties)

    Answer choice A is the only figure that has a line of symmetry. It is equal on both sides of a line drawn through the middle.

10. **A**   (Standard Assessed: Numerical Operations)

    Greg needs 80¢. The sum of three quarters is 75¢. If you add a nickel to that, you get 80¢. The coins in answer choice B add up to 75¢. The coins in answer choice C add up to 85¢. The coins in answer choice D add up to 60¢.

11. **D**   (Standard Assessed: Geometric Properties)

    Answer choice A is a line segment. Answer choice B is a ray. Answer choice C is an angle. Answer choice D is a line.

12. **D**   (Standard Assessed: Units of Measurement)

    If you wanted to measure a distance across town, which is very far, you would use miles. This is the largest unit of measurement.

13. Open-ended   (Standard Assessed: Patterns)

    **Sample answer:** Each day of the week, 3 more gallons of milk are sold. On Thursday, 14 gallons of milk were sold. If you add 3 to 14, you get 17. Seventeen gallons of milk would be sold on Friday.

14. **B**   (Standard Assessed: Geometric Properties)

    Congruent shapes are exactly the same. Answer choice B is the only answer choice that shows two shapes that are exactly the same.

15. **D** (Standard Assessed: Data Analysis)

After you find the bar for Test 5, move up to see what Eric's grade was. You can tell right away that it is higher than 80. Answer choice D is correct.

16. **B** (Standard Assessed: Data Analysis)

Ken has 📖 📖 📖 after his name. If you look at the key, it says that each 📖 stands for 2 books. So you need to multiply $3 \times 2$. Ken read 6 books.

17. **A** (Standard Assessed: Coordinate Geometry)

To find coordinates for Point *B*, count over 3 on the *x*-axis and then up 1. Answer choice A is correct.

18. **C** (Standard Assessed: Measurement of Geometrical Objects)

If you measure this line segment with the centimeter part of your ruler, you'll see that it is exactly 4 centimeters.

19. **B** (Standard Assessed: Combinations)

To find the combination, write down *tan pants* and *black pants*. Then put all (or both) jacket choices by each pair of pants. When you draw a line from each pair of pants to each jacket choice, you will have 4 lines.

20. **C** (Standard Assessed: Modeling)

To find the value of *p*, answer the question "What number subtracted from 16 equals 9?" The answer is 7.

21. **C** (Standard Assessed: Numerical Operations)

If you add the number of cars Sidney has, 32, 24, and 12, the answer is 68.

**22.** Open-ended   (Standard Assessed: Geometric Properties)

**Sample answer:** The first figure is a square. The second figure is a cube. A square has four corners, and a cube has eight.

The figures are the same in that they are shaped alike. They are different in that a square is two-dimensional and a cube is three-dimensional.

**23. C**   (Standard Assessed: Discrete Mathematics)

If you look at the parts of the circles that overlap, you'll see that the only answer choice that is true for both Mom and Dad is that they have brown eyes.

**24. B**   (Standard Assessed: Patterns)

The number 4 is in the *x* column and the number 1 is across from it in the *y* column. You have to subtract 3 from 4 to get 1. This is also true of the other numbers in the *x* column. You have to subtract 3 from each of them to get the number in the *y* column.

**25. C**   (Standard Assessed: Patterns)

For each number in the examples, 10 is subtracted before it comes out of the function machine. So, if 20 is dropped into the machine, it will come out as 10.

**26. C**   (Standard Assessed: Probability)

There are 20 beads altogether, and 5 of these beads are pink. If Carmen reaches into the bag without looking, there is a 5 out of 20 chance that she will pull out a pink bead.

**27. D**   (Standard Assessed: Modeling)

To find the number that should go in the box, answer the question "What must be added to 13 to get 20?"

**28. C**   (Standard Assessed: Patterns)

Each of the input column numbers is multiplied by 2 to get the output column numbers. For example, $6 \times 2 = 12$.

**29. B**  (Standard Assessed: Modeling)

Remember that any number multiplied by 0 is 0.

**30. A**  (Standard Assessed: Data Analysis)

If you look at the number across from Year 2, you'll see that it is 16.

**31.** Open-ended   (Standard Assessed: Data Analysis)

**Sample answer:** In January, there were 100 cars sold. In July, there were 400 cars sold. Car sales go up as the weather gets warmer.